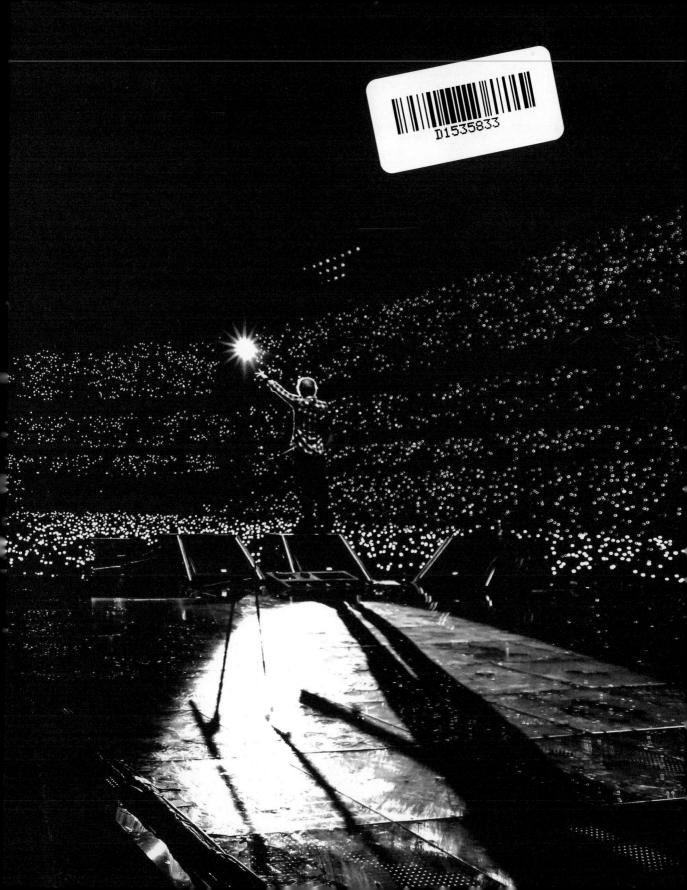

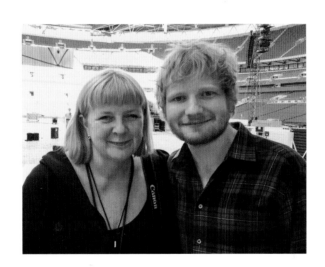

FOR HARRY SANDLER

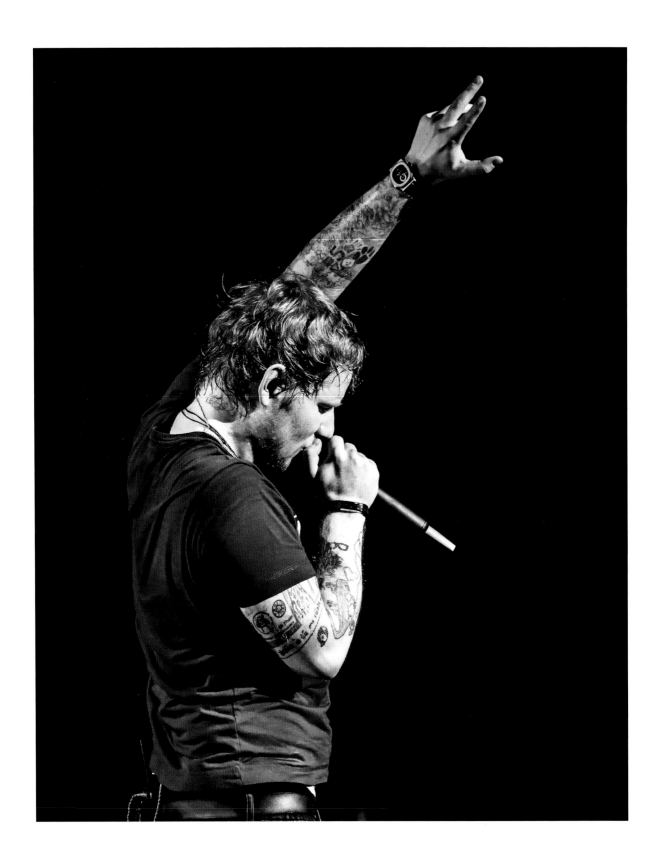

Ed Sheeran

MEMORIES WE MADE

UNSEEN PHOTOGRAPHS of my time with ED

CHRISTIE GOODWIN

Foreword by JOHN SHEERAN

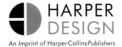

HARPER
DESIGN

An Imprint of HarperCollinsPublishers

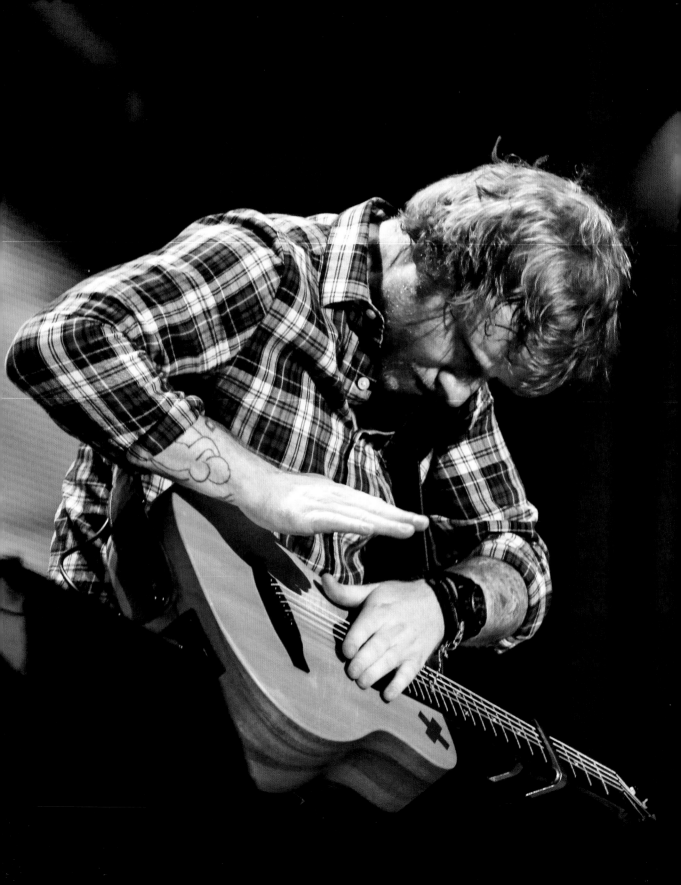

contents

—

foreword   7
JOHN SHEERAN

introduction   9
WHY I TAKE PICTURES

choosing pictures   13
HOW TO CREATE A BOOK

camden   19
MEETING ED

girl guides big gig   29
THANKS OLLY

shepherd's bush empire   35
THE THREE-SONG RULE

itunes festival   43
MEET YOU AT THE BEER KEGS

hammersmith apollo   63
THE PHOTO PASS DEBACLE

centurylink center   71
CONQUERING AMERICA

scottrade center   77
CHASING THE SCOOTER

john henry's studios   99
STUDIO SHOOT

teenage cancer trust   113
ROYAL ALBERT HALL DEBUT

the o2 arena   149
UNDER THE MILLENNIUM DOME

wembley stadium   155
WEMBLEY REHEARSALS
ED RULES WEMBLEY
CAPTURING THE ESSENCE OF ED

teenage cancer trust II   201
ON MY TURF AGAIN

afterword   217
THE DIRTY TRUTH

about the authors   222

thank you   224

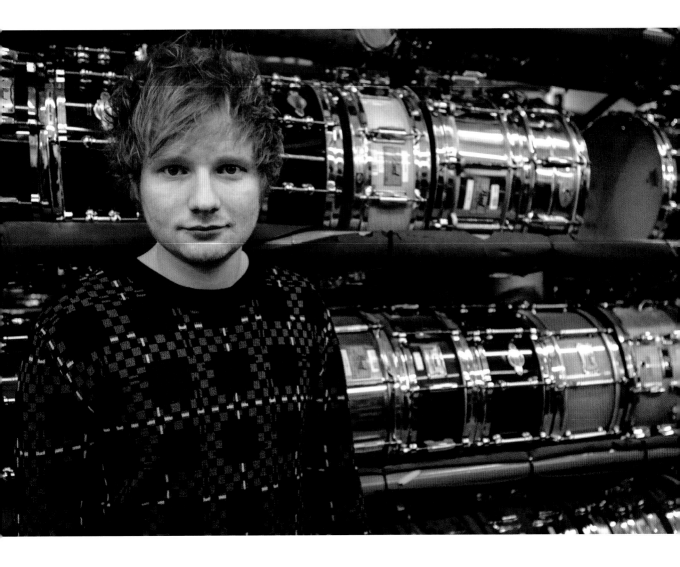

foreword

— JOHN SHEERAN —

My wife, Imogen, and I first met the music photographer Christie Goodwin, and her partner and manager Patrick Cusse, one evening in February 2008 at The Enterprise pub in Camden. We had driven to London from Suffolk with our son Ed, who had just turned 17. He was due to play as a support act in an upstairs room of the pub. We wanted to help Ed as much as we could, but were both clueless about the music industry and London music scene, and how it all worked. Now, for the first time, we were meeting real professionals. And they were both so kind and caring to Ed. Christie had agreed to shoot photos of Ed performing for free – his first ever professional images. I remember how excited we both were about that.

The gig turned out to be a bit of a disaster as the electrics cut out after a few minutes and Ed had to play unplugged, but typically he won over the 20 or so people in the room; I was disappointed however, as I thought there was no way that Christie could have come away with any decent shots of Ed. How wrong I was. I later saw her photos and was amazed. She had managed to get a series of headshots that made our inexperienced son look like a veteran of his craft.

Now here we are, ten years on. Ed is at the top of his game, and so is Christie. Imogen and I feel so proud of them both. They have worked so hard to achieve their success, and it hasn't been easy. Ed did hundreds of gigs in London and around the UK, sleeping on sofas and selling CDs from his rucksack, before he got his break. And you only need to read what Christie has written in this book to understand just how tough the journey has been for her, too.

I love the fact that Ed and Christie both started in pubs and clubs, and are now doing arenas and stadiums. So I see this book as a wonderful celebration of their creative talents, strengths of character and professionalism. Thank you, Christie and Patrick, for asking me to become involved. It has been a privilege. Good luck with everything you do in the future.

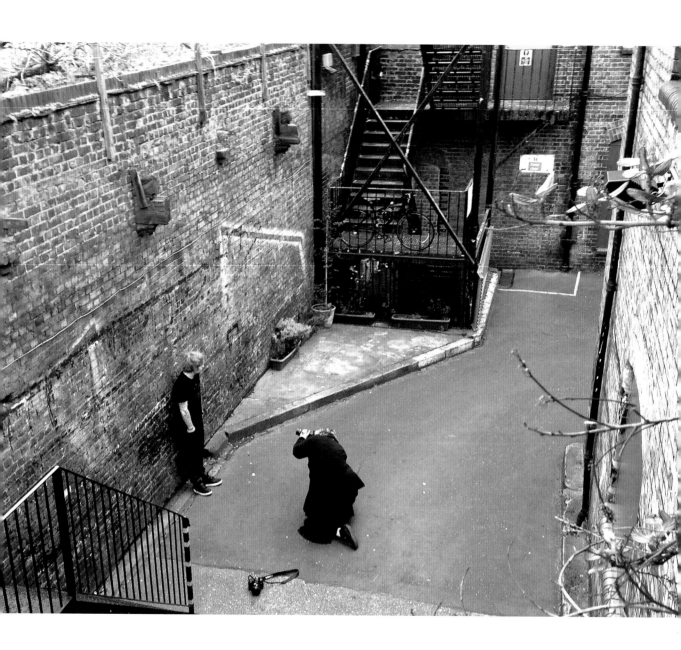

introduction

▬▬▬

I remember as a very young child – I must have been three or four years old – I used to stay at my grandad's house where he had these hefty leather-bound photo albums, filled with old black-and-white photos. They were stuck to thick black pages and there were these flimsy thin dividers between the pages. You always had to be really careful to put those dividers nicely flat or you would crinkle up the whole sheet.

One of the most intriguing photographs in his collection was one of my grandfather and grandmother walking down the street. Next to my grandmother was her sister, and a little behind her was her sister's husband. It must have been the 1950s and taken by an anonymous street photographer. It was common practice back then for photographers to take pictures of people walking on the street and then hand them their card so they could go to look at the picture once it had been developed and, with any luck, buy it from them. I guess it must have been quite a solid marketing strategy because my grandfather went and bought that picture and eventually stuck it in one of his albums.

My grandfather, grandmother and her sister were all three of them looking straight into the lens of the photographer's camera; the sister's husband, by contrast, was looking down while inhaling the smoke from his cigarette. There was something about that picture that mesmerized me. I remember sitting on this big old sofa with this oversized album carefully placed on top of my little legs and just staring at that photo, looking very hard to see if I had missed anything; wondering what they were doing, where they were going and where they were coming from. Were they happy or were they sad? And why was the sister's husband not looking into the camera? So many questions, so many things I wanted to know just by looking at that picture.

It's that simplicity and the invitation to the world inside the image that to this day I still try to bring into my own work. The magic for me happens as soon as I look through the viewfinder. I actually very much enjoy that the frame of the viewfinder restrains me. I like to fit things into the frame, be it rectangular or square, depending on what you are shooting with. But I feel safe and comfortable within the constraints of the viewfinder. That's my world and I can compose it, fill it up like I want. I prefer my frame not too filled up; I hate clutter in my frame and I love lots of breathing space within the borders.

The biggest challenge for me today after shooting pictures for more than 35 years is to walk into an assignment and find something that inspires me to dig my heels in, so I can bring a bit of magic into a frame. It's not always that easy because sometimes I get an assignment where the music is totally not my cup of tea, or sometimes the artist is a really big character whose larger-than-life attitude makes it difficult to find something appealing to capture. But shooting Ed Sheeran is different. Although I would love his stages to be a bit lower, and it would be nice if we had a little less clutter onstage (his two microphone stands can get in the way), taking photos of Ed is easy for me. For starters, his music is very captivating, almost addictive. His stage presence, too, is energetic and tireless, moving swiftly from the very solemn to the peppy and vivacious. Ed brings a whole spectrum of emotions to every show, and they are raw and authentic. I have often said this, but I don't understand how anyone could take a bad picture of Ed. If you observe him performing, and you are guided by his music and his passion and enthusiasm, then it is almost impossible to take a bad picture of him. I've grown very protective of Ed and of the images of him that are out there. When I see a picture of Ed that doesn't look good or that doesn't have the depth I feel is appropriate for Ed, I can get really annoyed.

If you look through the relatively short history of music photography, you will notice that what people call great music pictures are often photos of artists before they became famous, or in the early days of their fame. There is an excitement when you look at a picture with the knowledge you have of where that person is now. It's almost like you know the ending of a book but you are still reading it from the start. Over the decade that I have shot Ed, I have been privileged to be able to pop into his bubble on a few occasions and be a quiet witness to his rise to success. He is as determined as they come. And as weird as it may sound talking about someone who fills football stadiums, I truly believe this is only the beginning.

Many of my photos of Ed were taken before the football stadiums, and I hope you enjoy looking back at Ed's history as much as I have putting this book together. Moments in life are fleeting: time passes by so quickly and everything around us is constantly changing. I think that is why photography is so important. It allows us to hold on to those moments but also to remember them as time passes us by. My first shoot with Ed back in 2008 might have been insignificant to him at that time. Ed probably didn't care about what I was shooting because I just popped into his life for a millisecond and then I was gone again. Today those pictures have become some of those rare early-day pictures of a very successful artist. The importance of those images has shifted because we now know what happened after. The world's most iconic photographs were captured in an instant, but they invited us in to create stories around them that are still being told today. I always give the example of Jimi Hendrix burning his guitar at the Monterey International Pop Festival in June 1967. It has stood the test of time. The photo was taken by Ed Caraeff and ended up on the cover of *Rolling Stone* twice. Hendrix setting his Fender Stratocaster on fire was just the epitome of rock 'n' roll. It was the era where rock stars were known to throw TVs out of their hotel windows. That picture was visible proof of the debauchery of rock stars of that time. Generation after generation can still witness that extraordinary moment. Even people who have never heard of Jimi Hendrix or heard his music still can see that he doused a guitar in lighter fluid and set it ablaze. The photo keeps the story alive. By recording that moment in history, Caraeff has allowed that iconic act to become eternal.

By the same token, every picture I have taken of Ed are all utterly small fragments of his timeline. I was just there to keep the stories alive. Consider me as your witness when you couldn't be there. And, if you were there, then maybe one day you can share these images with your children and tell them: "I was there". That's when I'll know that I have succeeded in my mission.

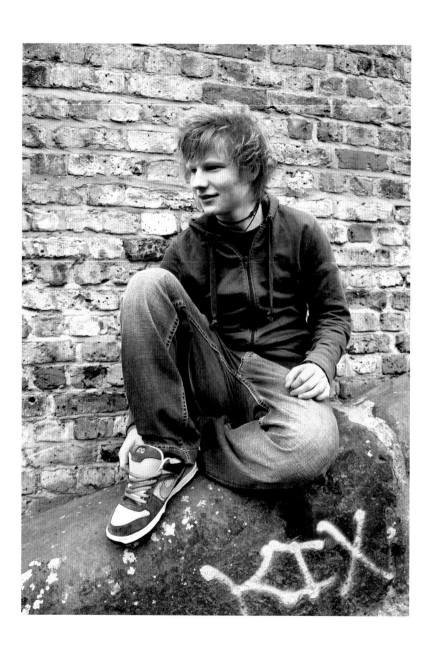

choosing pictures

Over the years my partner and manager Patrick Cusse had often toyed with the idea of doing a book with my work but it had never gone further than that. I met Patrick in 2004. He was a newspaper sports editor at the time, but he had a passion for photography. A year later we started working together.

I've never really felt the need to do a book because I prefer to look forward to my next shoot; I'm not generally fond of looking back. But Patrick wouldn't give up. Getting me to do a book with my pictures was on his bucket list. When the literary agent Carrie Kania suggested I do a book with my photos of Ed Sheeran all the pieces fell into place so quickly: Carrie became my book agent, meetings with Octopus Publishing were set up, and John Sheeran, Ed's father, offered to help me choose the photos. So, I said yes and signed my name on the dotted line.

Then reality hit me hard. The fact is that I've never really had to choose which of my pictures should be published and I had never created a book before. I didn't know the first thing about what it takes. I usually shoot pictures for a client and I know what the client expects from me. Some clients will use my work to promote upcoming shows, others might use my work on the packaging and booklet of a DVD; often, some shots end up on a T-shirt or in a calendar. I deliver a tight selection of pictures and from then on it's up to the client what happens to them. The burden of making that final and important selection is up to them.

My archive of Ed Sheeran holds more than 2,000 pictures. That was my starting point. My first mission was to choose a manageable number to start from. It took me a good few days to plough through them all, and it turned out to be much more difficult than I thought it would be. Somehow you have to get your head around what would work in a book: each photo has to showcase Ed at some key moment in his career, but all the while tell a story. One day I would have a selection in place that I thought could work, and the next day I already hated the lot of them.

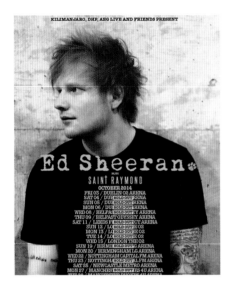

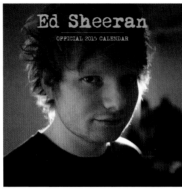

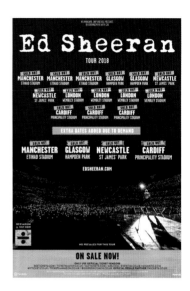

It was obvious that I didn't really know how to select my own work. I managed to get the 2,000 pictures down to a collection of 600 and that was as far as I got. I recognized that I needed help to eliminate another three-quarters from that.

I reached out to John Sheeran. John's not just Ed's dad: he has extensive experience creating art books and curating exhibitions worldwide, so I was confident he would be able to guide me through the process. John kindly took me under his wing and gave me extraordinary advice throughout the whole procedure.

My work is profoundly personal to me. I shoot pictures of what I experience, and I put a lot of myself into what I create. So, to have an outsider put your work under a magnifying glass and critique it in your presence is immensely hard. But John knows his job, and his brutal honesty feels almost comforting. I have to admit that for someone who is super sensitive about sharing their work, I stunned myself by how easy it was to share my work with John, take in his advice and listen to his critique. Because he knows Ed so well, he could easily pinpoint certain facets of Ed's performances that needed to be included in the book, some of which I hadn't realized that I had actually captured.

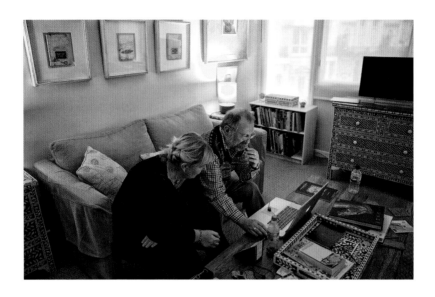

No matter how many technically perfect pictures you have in your catalogue, it's not until you have to narrow them down and put them in context that they actually come to life. John took a few days to narrow down the selection to just under 200 pictures. We then met up one morning and spent a good few hours going over that selection. John repeatedly challenged me to react instinctively to whether a picture worked or not. I surprised myself on how harshly my gut would respond when put in that position. And soon enough it all started to come together.

John set the bar quite high because he wanted to bring out the very best of me. He had a list of boxes that the photos needed to tick: photos that are superb in terms of their composition, colour, lighting and so on; photos that tell stories; photos that show what's unique about Ed – his character, talent, drive, ambition, performance, presence and skills; photos that capture the experience of the audience and the specific atmosphere of a particular show; and photos that show off my art and craft. You could say that I learned how to select my own pictures from Ed's dad. If I take anything out of creating this book, it is most certainly that.

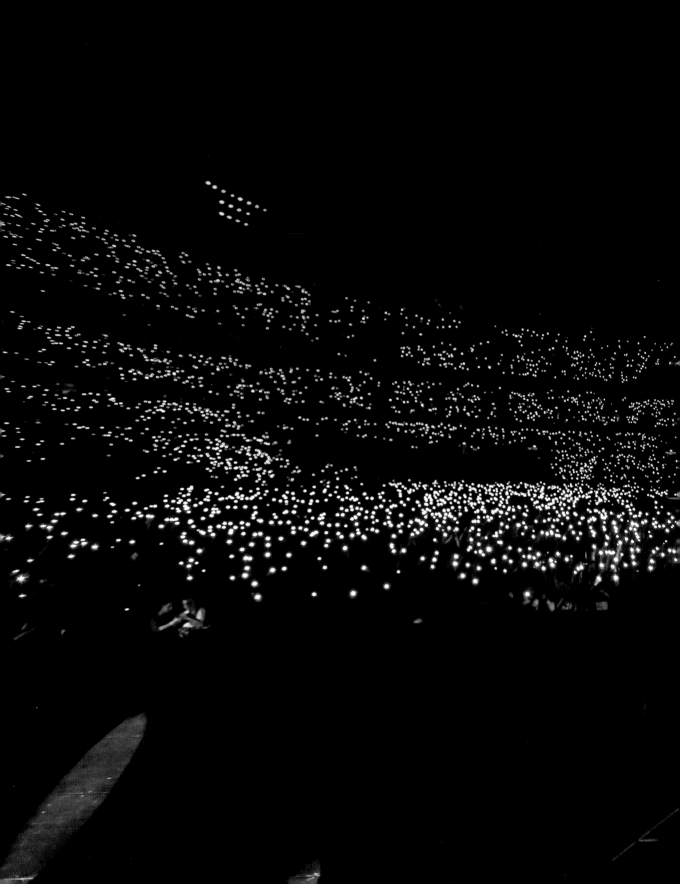

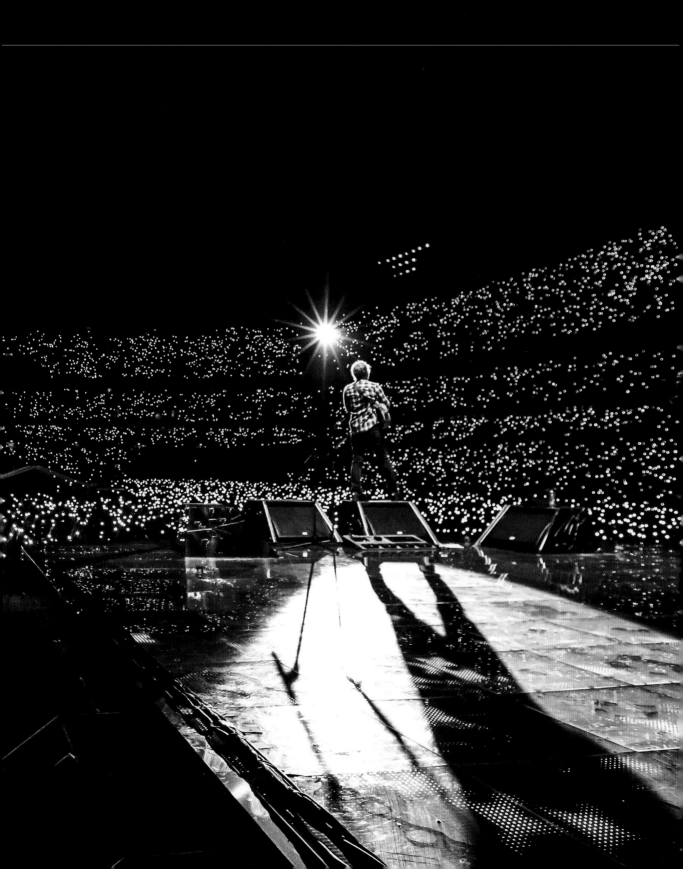

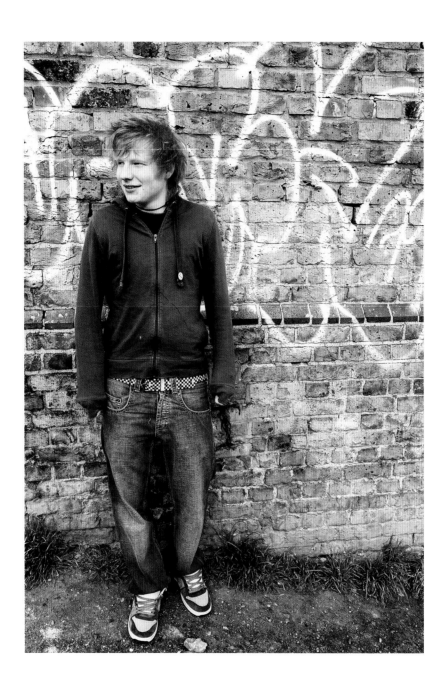

camden

▬

MEETING ED

It all began by chance. It was February 2008 and it had only been a couple of years since I had gone from shooting editorial work to music photography. I was in the process of building up a portfolio that could represent my work in the music industry. That meant that I shot what I could, where I could, which was often in pubs, clubs and small venues. And even though my policy has always been to never shoot without being paid, as it undermines the industry, when you are still building up your portfolio at times you will find it's necessary to bend that rule.

One of the doors I had been knocking on was that of Crown Music, a management company that was pretty good at spotting new talent. They had just taken on this kid with a guitar named Ed Sheeran and they had sent me a couple of links to him. I thought he'd be a good fit for my portfolio, so I accepted the job. A portrait shoot in the afternoon and a gig in the evening, both in Camden, north London.

When the day came, I found myself down and out with a serious stomach bug. It was evident that there was no way I would be able to travel into London and do the shoot. Either I had to cancel, or go to plan B. That morning I gave Patrick, my manager and partner, a crash course in how to use my camera, what to look for and how to capture it, and gave him a little checklist of what kind of material I wanted to see him come back with.

While I was ill at home, Patrick met Ed around noon in Camden. They spent an hour walking around Camden Lock and Patrick shot some casual portraits following my instructions. Ed had brought a small and strangely shaped guitar as a prop. Afterward, Patrick returned home and showed me the pictures. I carefully

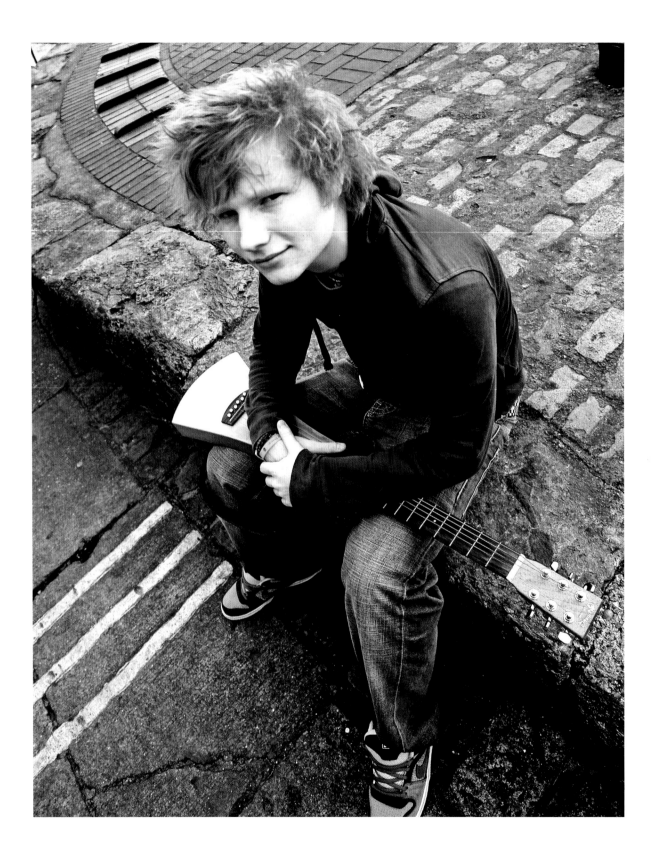

John Sheeran

Here is Ed in early 2008, a few days after his seventeenth birthday, at Camden Lock, London. He is posing for some free publicity shots taken by Patrick Cusse under the guidance of Christie. He looks fresh-faced and innocent, just one of hundreds of aspiring young singers and musicians, most older than him, playing the circuit of pubs and clubs at the time. He looks up quizzically, resting on his trusted backpacker guitar, which went everywhere with him, usually stuffed into his rucksack along with self-produced CDs, which he sold at gigs to pay for his food. It's extraordinary to think that only eight years later he would be selling out three nights at Wembley Stadium.

selected the best of what he had managed to capture and edited them in my usual style. We were left with a good handful of portraits. But, more importantly, Patrick had been really enthusiastic about Ed. He seemed to really like him. Patrick's enthusiasm made me dead set on getting to the gig that night, no matter what.

I bit the bullet and we set off to London. I vividly recall getting on the London Underground heading for Chalk Farm station when I started to feel really queasy, and halfway there it was just getting worse. There was a real moment I thought I was not going to make it. Patrick reminded me casually that we didn't really have to do the shoot, as it wasn't actually a paid commission. It was really more of a favour to this young kid playing clubs. I was determined to see it through. I decided to just brave it and do the shoot as I had agreed. This just shows how seemingly insignificant decisions we make in an instant at any given time can sometimes become so much more significant over time.

Ed was the opening act at a gig at The Enterprise in Camden. The Enterprise was an old-school indie boozer just across the road from the then newly refurbished Roundhouse performance venue. It's still there, but it looks quite different these days. Upstairs, they had a small club room for gigs. I remember climbing up the stairs and entering this dark room, with a small and pretty basic podium at the end. We spotted Ed setting up his gear, and we walked over and shook hands. He introduced us to his dad John and his mother Imogen, and then continued setting up. We had a friendly casual chat with Ed's parents. John explained to us that Ed had been gigging as much as he could and was trying to build up a following. He hadn't secured a record deal yet but that was what he was working toward. I loved how supportive his parents were.

About an hour or so later a small crowd of maybe 20 to 25 people had gathered in the room. Ed took to the stage and started his performance. The lights, however, were pretty much non-existent, which isn't unusual for small clubs. There was one small orange spotlight on his face and that's all I had to work with. I couldn't properly capture his guitar or anything else, even if my life had depended on it. That is the main reason why I have only a couple of very tight facial shots from that first performance I shot of Ed. And things were about to get worse.

A couple of songs into the show there was a sudden power cut at the club. There was a slight moment of panic as everything went dark. Someone from

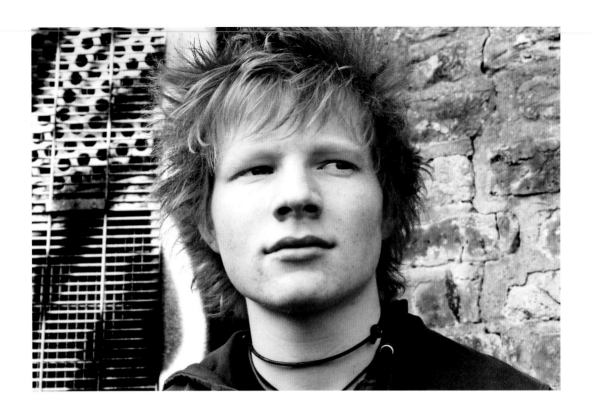
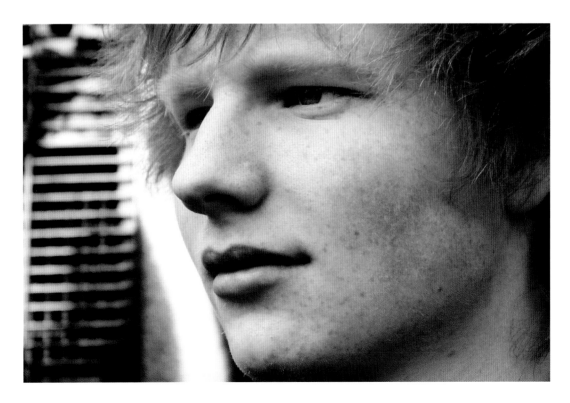

the venue said they would try to fix it as fast as they could. The room filled with chatter. People just went on with their evening, waiting, probably thinking that was it as far as the support act was concerned. I noticed Ed unplugging his gear and I assumed he was packing in for the night. But, to everyone's surprise, Ed instead walked to the front of the stage, moved the mic stand out of the way and announced that the remainder of his performance would be unplugged. The chatter in the room silenced, Ed took his guitar, looked into the crowd and asked if anyone wanted to volunteer to accompany him doing the beats to his songs. A young guy, who was actually the main act later that evening, got up and said to Ed, "I'll do it." He walked up on to the stage with a box. He tapped on the box while Ed played his acoustic guitar. Ed finished his set, much to the audience's delight. Like a seasoned professional, he had made a split-second decision. He didn't panic but instead turned this technical breakdown into a fabulous unplugged performance.

Because all this happened pretty much in complete darkness, I couldn't capture anything of that (and, before you ask, no, I didn't bring my flashgun that night because I don't do flash photography – it's against my religion), but I did stay and enjoyed the performance all the same. It was fascinating to witness. It might sound cheesy looking back at it now, but there was something special about Ed and how he just overcame that hurdle.

When putting together this book I thought of digging up my old diaries to see what I had entered for that day I first met Ed. Interestingly, I didn't write anything about sending Patrick on a portrait shoot that afternoon. Nor did I mention that I spent most of the day ill. Instead, there was just a very short but quite prophetic entry:

"What can I say about Ed? Ed Sheeran is a 17-year-old singer-songwriter from East Anglia, that's what his dad told me. The gig I experienced with him was quite something. Halfway through his set his gear just went 'pffft'. Ed unplugged his guitar and continued his thing without the amp and without the mic. Shows this kid can do it alright. So, here's news for you, watch this kid. He has charisma, he is likeable and cute. All he needs is some catchy tunes and he'll be there at the top of the bill in the very near future. Tell everyone I said so."

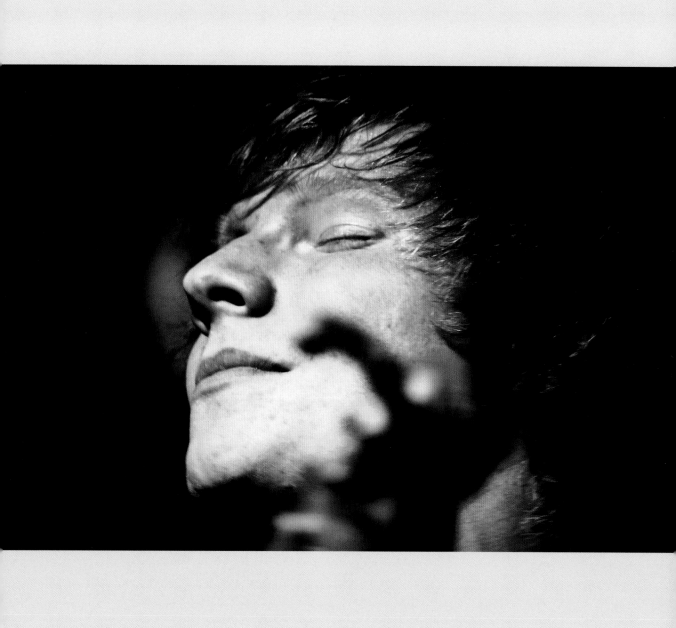

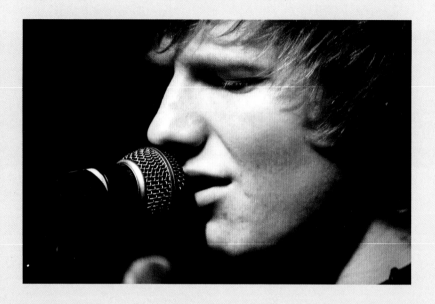

John Sheeran

These headshots were taken during a gig in an upstairs room of The Enterprise pub in
Camden, a few hours after the Camden Lock photoshoot, in February 2008. They are the
first professional photos taken of Ed performing. Just after he started singing, there was
an electrical fault and his microphone, guitar and loop pedal all failed, but despite that
he continued. Given the difficult circumstances, Christie still managed to get powerfully
expressive images of the intensity of feeling in Ed's performance. They make an artist in
the infancy of his career look like a seasoned professional. Ed went on to do hundreds of
more gigs, mostly unpaid like this one, before an artist management company, Rocket,
picked up on him.

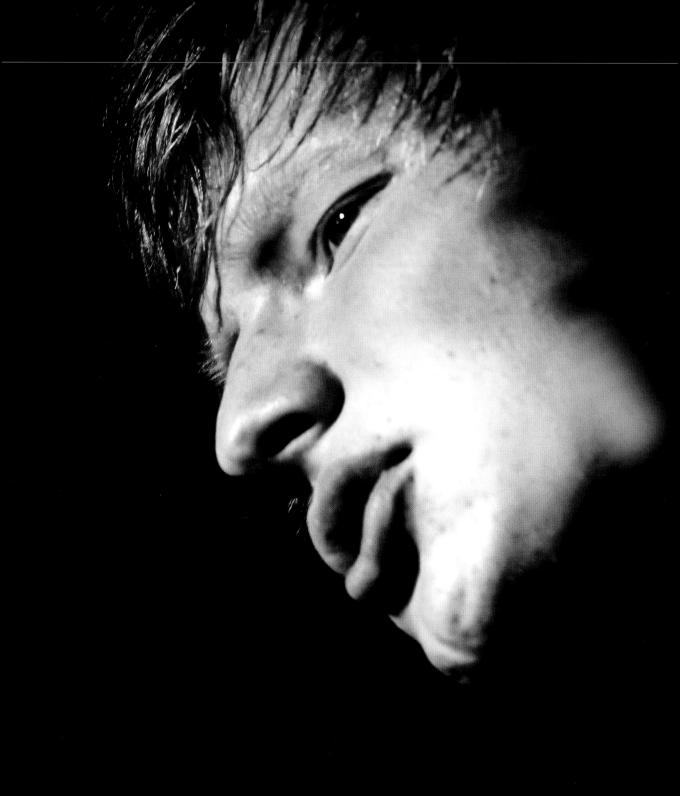

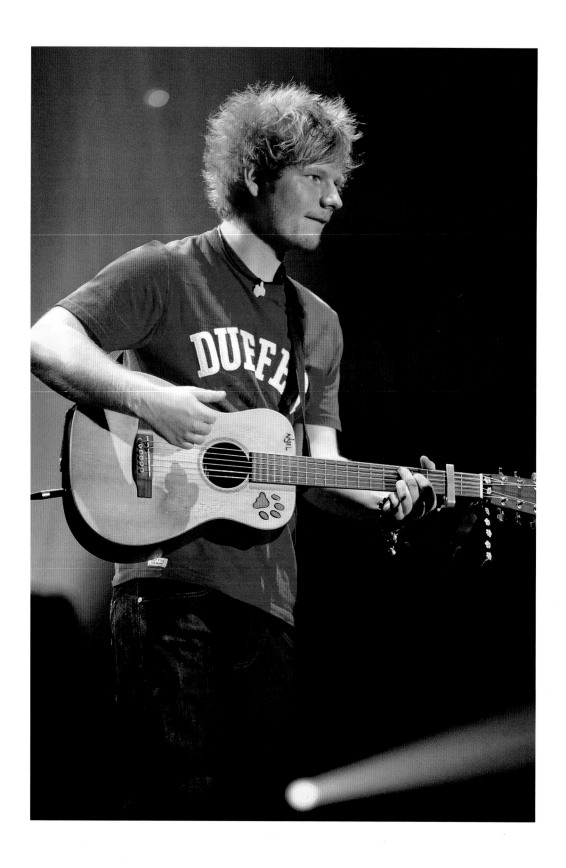

girl guides big gig

THANKS OLLY

It was about three years after I first met Ed at The Enterprise in Camden that I ran into him again, totally unexpectedly. I was still freelancing at that time, building up my portfolio and shooting as many gigs as I could get my hands on. By now I often contributed to Redferns/Getty Images, an editorial photo agency that supplies concert and other editorial photos to the media.

On Saturday, 1 October 2011, I was assigned to cover the annual Girl Guides Big Gig for Getty Images at Wembley Arena in London. The Big Gig is always a good one to shoot because they consistently have a good line-up of young acts well on their way to the top. As per usual, the Big Gig consisted of two shows in one day, one in the afternoon and one in the evening. I was shooting the afternoon show. I hadn't paid much attention to the line-up aside from the slightly bigger names at that time, like The Wanted, Olly Murs and Pixie Lott. I wasn't aware that Ed was performing that afternoon.

The routine shooting the Big Gig was that each act would perform a couple of songs, which I would shoot from the pit. After their performance the act would pop up backstage in the media room where press photographers could shoot a couple of quick portraits in front of a branding board, before they would be absorbed by bloggers and journalists doing interviews with them. As a photographer covering this type of event you have to run yourself silly, and you know in advance you'll never get it all covered. There are two flights of stairs and a couple of corridors between the pit and the branding board. I couldn't be in two places at once, so occasionally I had to set priorities. For my portfolio, I was after the performance shots. But as I was shooting for press that afternoon I knew I definitely had to get the portraits, as agencies like to push those more

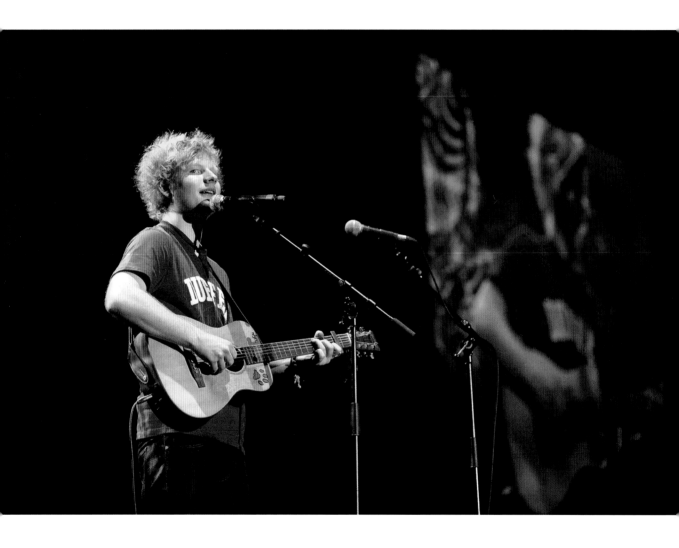

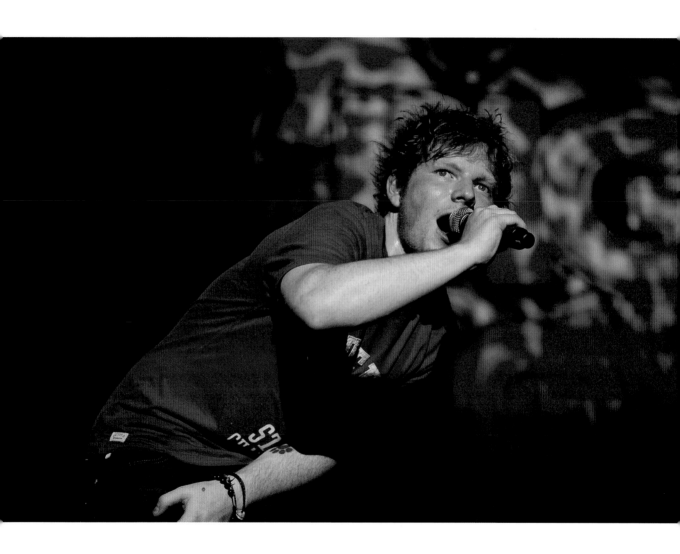

than live shots. You see my dilemma? I was especially keen to get a good portrait of Olly Murs. He had been making some waves since performing on the UK's *The X-Factor* in 2009.

After Olly's performance, I was dashing back to the media room when I got blocked by catering staff coming down the stairs carrying large crates of wine glasses. There was simply no way through; they were taking up the whole width of the staircase. I had to wait patiently for them to arrive at the bottom of the stairs before I could rush my way up. It had cost me only about a minute, but it was enough. As I reached the media room completely out of breath, Olly had already finished his portrait session at the board. I scanned the room and found Olly cozied up on a sofa giving an interview to one of the bloggers. I was gutted!

People who know me will tell you that when I want something I am like a bulldog, so I definitely wasn't going to throw in the towel just yet. I resolved to wait it out and be ready for the moment Olly rotated from one interview to another interview, then I would jump in and ask him if I could still have a quick shot looking into my camera. So, I parked myself on a sofa opposite him and watched him like a hawk. I got distracted when from the side of my eye I saw flashes firing from the direction of the branding board. I leaned over to try and get a glimpse of who the photographers were shooting. And there he was – Ed Sheeran.

I couldn't believe my eyes. Ed had just released his first album and it had gone straight to number one. And now he was here promoting himself. And so, another dilemma. Should I abandon my chase to get that shot of Olly and go over to say hi to Ed, or should I just stay put and keep my eyes on the prize?

While I deliberated my next move, the flashguns stopped firing and I saw Ed walking away from the board. For a moment, he was just standing there all by himself and it was apparent that he was waiting for a journalist to become available to interview him. Meanwhile, opposite me sat Olly, still happily chatting to the blogger, and that didn't seem to be ending any time soon. So, I got up and walked over to Ed and reintroduced myself. I didn't really think he would remember me. It had been quite a long three years since we first met, and that encounter had been such a short one as well. I politely stretched out my hand and said, "Hi there, you might not remember me but I shot you a couple of years ago in

Camden." He totally ignored my outstretched hand and instead just swung his arms around me and gave me a big hug. "Of course I remember you and Patrick. It was at The Enterprise." Well, that sure broke the ice. We had a bit of small talk and I seized the opportunity to take a quick portrait shot of him against the board because I had missed my opportunity earlier while I was waiting for Olly. He gallantly obliged, I thanked him, we hugged again. Before I left, Ed said, "We should have another shoot. Have Patrick drop me an email."

And Olly? Well, I never got that shot of Olly looking into my camera that afternoon. When I left Ed at the board, I looked back to where Olly had been sitting. He had already gone. Most likely he had finished his interviews and had been escorted back to the dressing rooms. You can't win them all, and while I was gutted about missing Olly, I felt quite good about reconnecting with Ed. And he was true to his word: we'd have another shoot, in fact more than one, in the years that followed.

And in the end I did get my portraits of Olly, too. In 2015 Olly hired me to go on tour with him for the behind-the-scenes photos in his book *On the Road*, and he has been a returning client ever since. I suppose there's a lesson in there somewhere. Never give up hope. One day everything will fall into place, as long as you're determined enough.

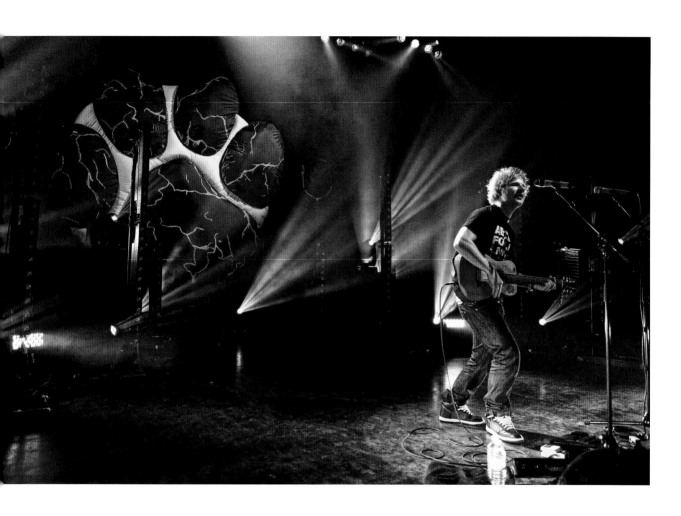

shepherd's bush empire

— LONDON, 3 OCTOBER 2011 —

John Sheeran

This is one of my favourite photos of Ed. We have it framed at home, outside his bedroom. In January 2006, when he was 15, I took Ed to the Shepherd's Bush Empire to see the band Nizlopi, who had recently had a number one hit with the "JCB Song". Driving back to Suffolk, Ed said that it would be his dream to play at Shepherd's Bush. I told him that, if he worked hard enough, one day he would headline there. So that became his ambition and his measure for success. And here he is five years later as the headline act, living his dream. You can see his cat paw print logo enlarged in the background, and the stage is dramatically lit with his favourite colour scheme of orange and black. Even his microphones are in these colours. The atmosphere that night was electric, with the crowd going crazy. Christie's dynamic shot captures for me the moment Ed burst on to the UK music scene.

35

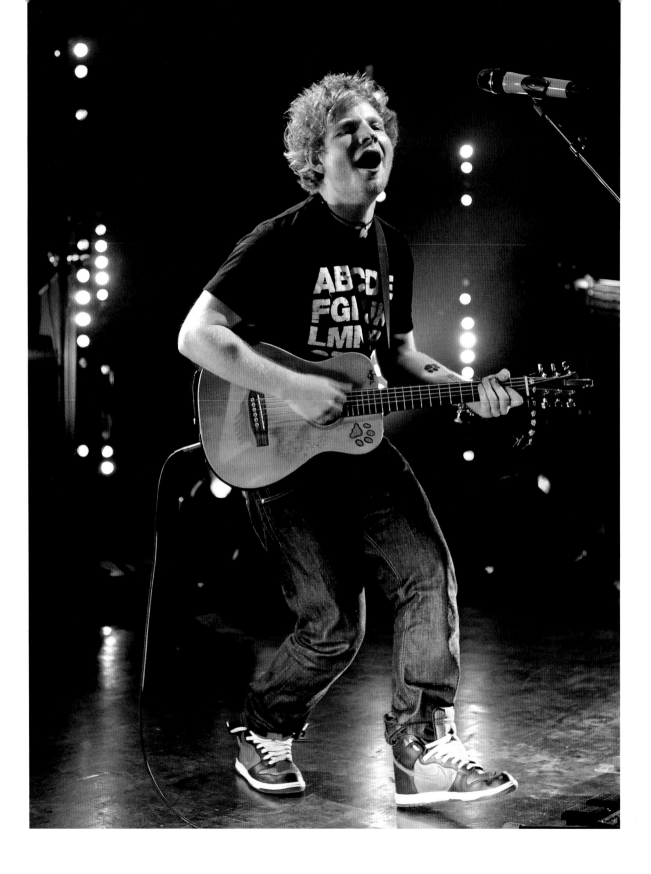

THE THREE-SONG RULE

Just two days after I had run into Ed at Wembley Arena, I was assigned to shoot Ed again for press. This time he was headlining his own proper show at Shepherd's Bush Empire in west London. Shepherd's Bush is a charming Grade II listed building, over a hundred years old. It holds about 2,000 people. Initially it was mainly a music hall, until the BBC bought it in the 1950s and filmed dozens of TV shows there. One of my all-time heroes, Terry Wogan, hosted his talk show there. In the 1990s it returned to its origins and has been a concert venue since.

I've always liked shooting at Shepherd's Bush because there is something very intimate about the layout of the venue. The way the crowd forms almost a semi-circle around the stage and the balconies come in really close is very inviting. The stage lights used at the venue are usually pretty decent, too, so I was really looking forward to this one.

I was covering the gig as a press photographer, which meant I would be shooting the first three songs of the performance only. I'm sure if you frequent concerts you might have noticed that the photographers who are in the pit shooting the performance get escorted out very early on. Please allow me to acquaint you with the "three-song rule", an unwritten rule followed worldwide by press photographers allowing them to photograph only the first three songs of a live show. There are several legends about the origin of this rule, but I favour this one.

By the 1980s artists were giving out huge numbers of photo passes to photographers, who were allowed to shoot from the pit and sometimes even to go onstage. Now, some of these photo passes were used by actual press photographers who would usually shoot only a couple of songs because they

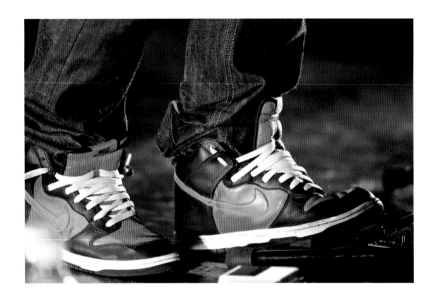

had tight deadlines to keep – they needed to get out, develop their film and submit their photos to the picture desks as soon as possible to make it into next day's paper. The rest of the photographers would be those shooting for magazines and the like, and had no deadlines, so they could stay for the whole show. Some of them would be using their flashguns throughout, which is probably the most annoying thing imaginable when you're onstage for two hours.

And the inevitable happened. Someone somewhere – legend has it that it was someone in Bruce Springsteen's entourage – decided that, if some photographers could get their shots in 15 minutes, then *all* of them could have their shots in 15 minutes. Quick maths: there's an average of five minutes to a song, thus three songs. To this day, this is still pretty much the rule for all press photographers worldwide. There are, as always, some exceptions to the rule. Some artists will push the limits even tighter, allowing press to shoot only one song, and very often they no longer even allow the photographers to shoot from the pit, but rather send them to the back of the arena near the soundboard so they are out of their sight. The weirdest one I have ever experienced myself was a high-profile artist who allowed the photographers to shoot only the first three seconds of their show. Yeah, you read that right: three *seconds*! Whether you agree or disagree with the concept of these imposed rules (and I disagree), the fact is that a photo pass is a privilege given by the artist. Still, it's a nonsensical rule when think about it, as you have thousands of fans who shoot/film entire performances on their smartphones and immediately share them on social media.

Anyway, back to that night in October 2011. As I arrived at the Shepherd's Bush Empire I went to collect my photo pass from the box office and walked back to the stage door, passing a horde of fans queuing outside. The long line of excited girls made me realize what kind of impact Ed was having, and that for him the days of a handful of punters in a club above a pub were long gone.

And there he was, Ed, with just a microphone, his guitar and his pedal board. From the very first notes he strummed he had the crowd in his hand. It was interesting to shoot him on a reasonably large stage with his own proper backdrop and his own lighting as well. After the first three songs, we all were escorted out of the pit, and I felt a bit thwarted because I got interrupted enjoying his performance. I'd seen Ed when he had first started out and I wanted to see him now on a bigger stage, the highlight of his career at that time.

I have, over the years, built good relationships with the different security teams at the various venues in London, including the security team of the Shepherd's Bush Empire. So when I asked them to let me back in without a camera to watch Ed conquer Shepherd's Bush, they let me in. I remember feeling really proud to see how far he'd come and how he commanded the crowd. Everyone was singing along to all his songs. I looked around and just about everyone knew the words to every single song he sang. He even got me going when toward the end of his set he orchestrated a singalong, splitting the crowd into two harmony groups. It was just exhilarating to watch him control the audience. I sang along with my side of the crowd as loud as I could. The whole of Shepherd's Bush was just on fire, and under a rapturous applause Ed jumped off stage and ran along the front row high-fiving everyone. I can only imagine how he must have felt that night. I left Shepherd's Bush on such a high. Ed was achieving everything and so much more than what he had set out to do.

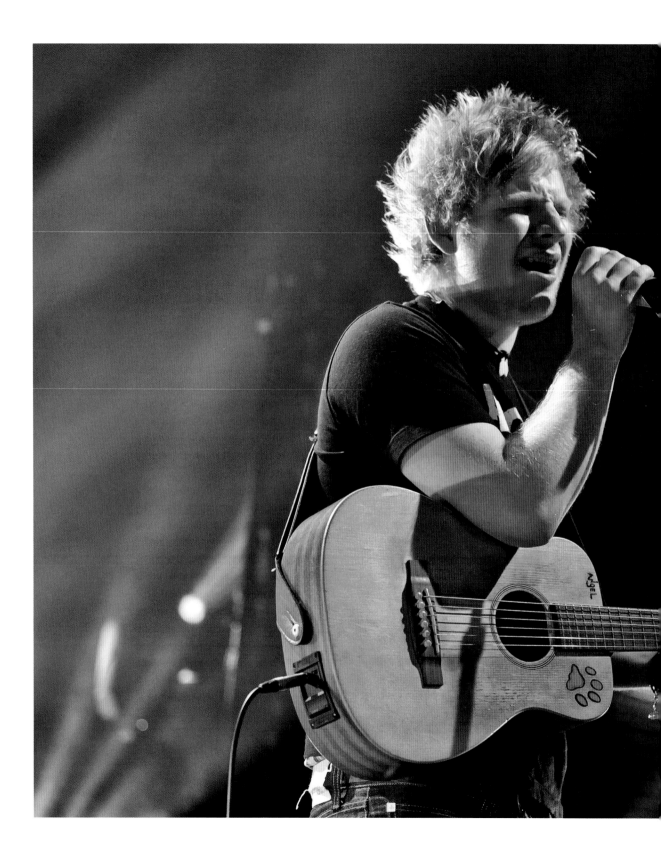

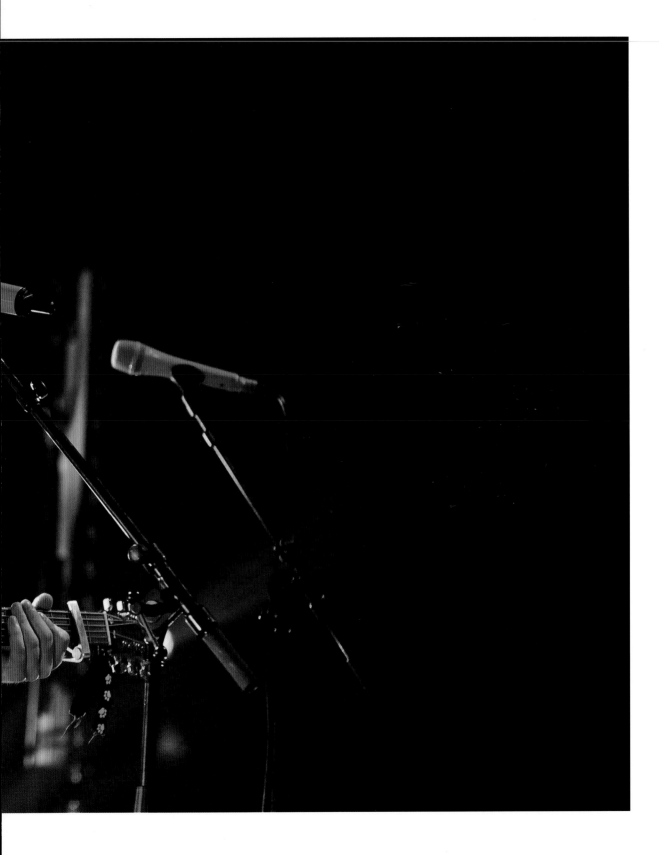

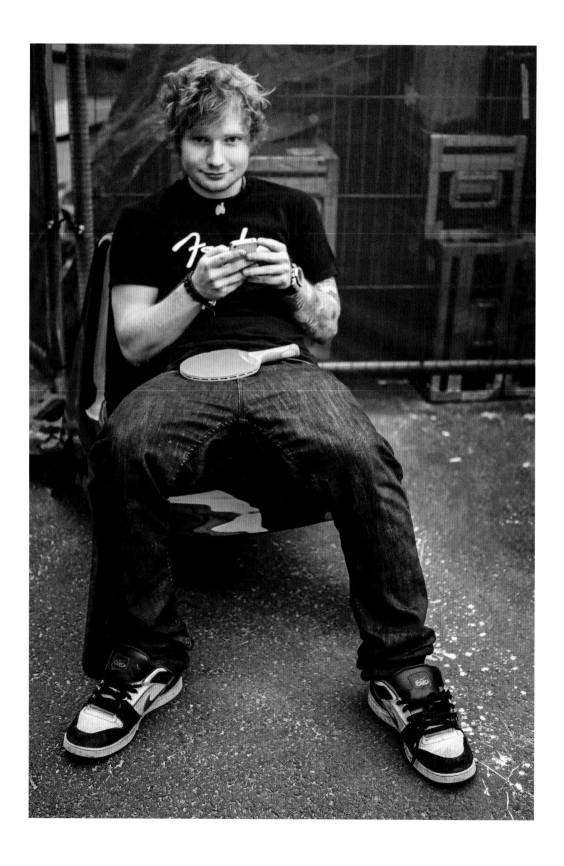

itunes festival

— THE ROUNDHOUSE, LONDON, 2 SEPTEMBER 2012 —

Christie Goodwin

Here is a candid shot of Ed backstage at the Roundhouse in London. Ed had been playing ping-pong with his tour manager, Mark Friend. My guess is that Mark probably had to go and sort something out, so Ed just sat back with his phone while waiting to resume the game with Mark. I love the cheeky look on his face in this picture.

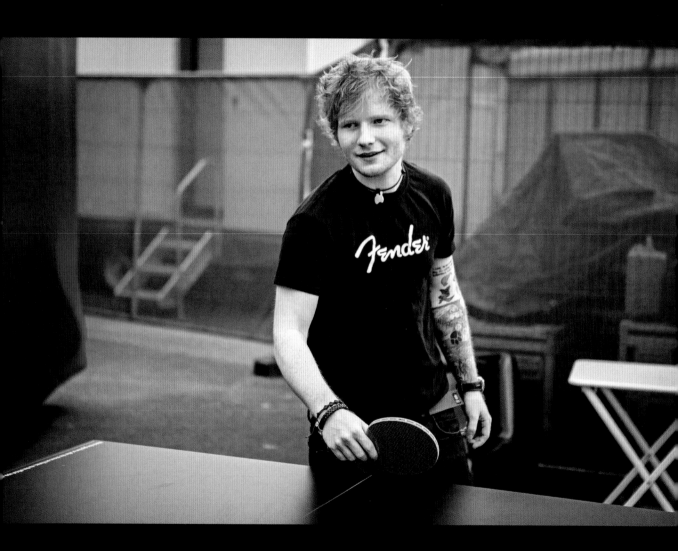

MEET YOU AT THE BEER KEGS

The iTunes Festival used to be an annual concert series during the month of September at the Roundhouse in Camden. The festival was very popular and quite unusual in that you couldn't actually buy your tickets. Instead, free tickets were given to iTunes users who lived in the United Kingdom through local prize draws. The concerts were streamed live via iTunes. The Roundhouse is another one of those iconic London buildings. It started life in the 19th century as an engine shed containing a railway turntable, became a warehouse and then a ruin, and to cut a long story short it finally reopened in 2006 as a concert venue.

On the second day of the 2012 iTunes Festival Charli XCX and Ed Sheeran were on the bill. I had been commissioned by the merchandising branch of Ed's record label. This was Ed being true to his word when I ran into him in 2011 and he said we would do a shoot together. At the time, the merchandising department needed urgent new shots to produce the Ed Sheeran 2013 calendar, and Ed had suggested they hire me. The brief was: backstage shots, a couple of portraits and the show.

There is this general misconception that bright sunlight will enable you to shoot a good picture. The truth is, though, that no photographer ever will jump in the air all excited and thrilled when stark bright sunbeams are hammering on the subject they have to shoot. It doesn't happen. Unless the sun is in context with a landscape, or you're working specifically with shadows, harsh sunlight is just a big no-no for photography.

Although that Sunday the weather forecast had promised scattered clouds, by the time we arrived at the Roundhouse the sun was blasting out. We met with Ed backstage and introduced ourselves to his manager, Stuart Camp. Elton

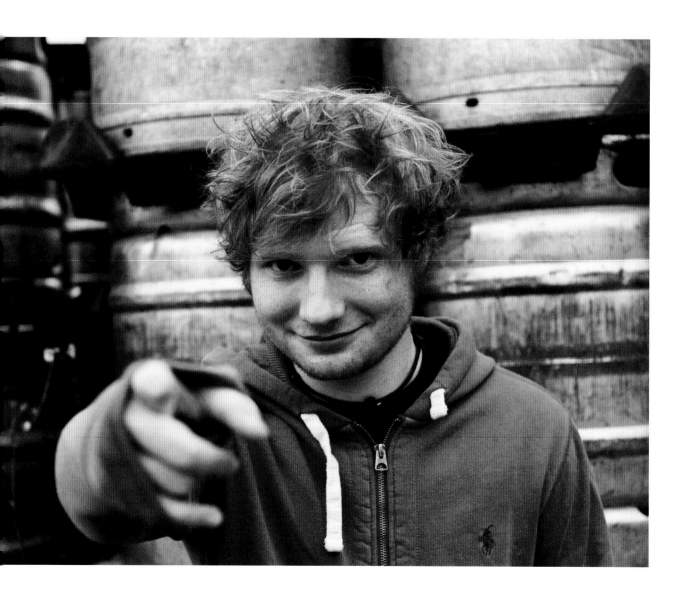

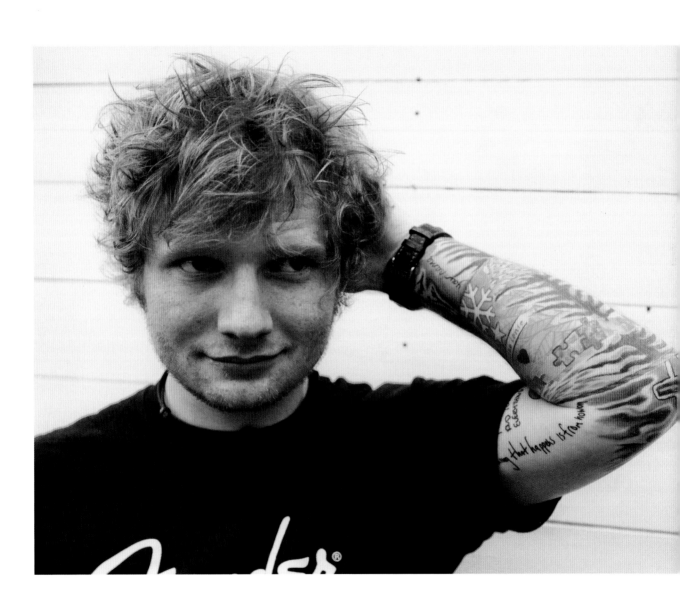

John's management company, Rocket, had signed Ed a while back, and this was the first time we had met Stuart and Ed's tour manager, Mark Friend. Over the years, Mark would always be a tremendous help to me, getting me where I needed to be to do my job, a tradition that he started on this day.

We went over the plan for the day. Everyone backstage was relaxed and upbeat because the sun was out and people kept telling me, "Look, we brought the sun out for you today so you can take excellent pictures." And all I wanted to do was just cry a bucketful of tears. Because of some logistic problems we had to push back the shoot while both Mark and Stuart were in constant negotiations with the iTunes people to get permission to use the outdoor backstage area for our photoshoot. By the time we got the green light it was already late afternoon and the sun was losing its strength. Yay me!

Once we got the go-ahead, I took Ed for a walk around the backstage area looking for backdrops that could work for our little portrait session. The options were limited as this was the backyard of a concert venue. It was mostly trailers, trucks and flight cases. And ... aluminium beer kegs. They seemed to draw Ed's interest so we started our session with a beer keg backdrop. Very urban.

I had spotted Ed's tattoos on his arm and I thought they were such a unique part of his identity. I wanted to create a shot where your eyes would immediately meet the tattoos when looking at the picture. I asked Ed if he was planning to get any more, and he told me he was in it for the long haul and had a list of ideas he still wanted to work out on his arms. That's when I suggested we should do some shots with him holding his tattooed arm up over his head. He wasn't sold on the idea and told me he didn't feel comfortable putting up his arm awkwardly without a purpose. But I knew there was something there, so I suggested that it would be merely documenting the development of his tattoos. In the end, he went along with my idea and those pictures I took that afternoon were some of the first where his tattoos were dominantly shown in an image.

Back at the lounge area that was set up for the artists, Ed picked up a game of ping-pong with Mark while I just continued casually shooting. I shot a whole sequence of impromptu pictures of Ed that afternoon, enough material to satisfy the merchandising team. And then it was showtime.

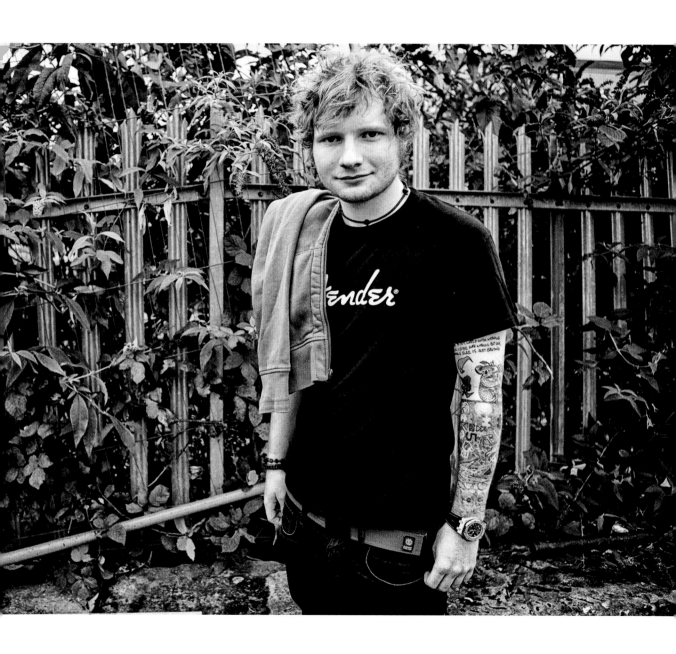

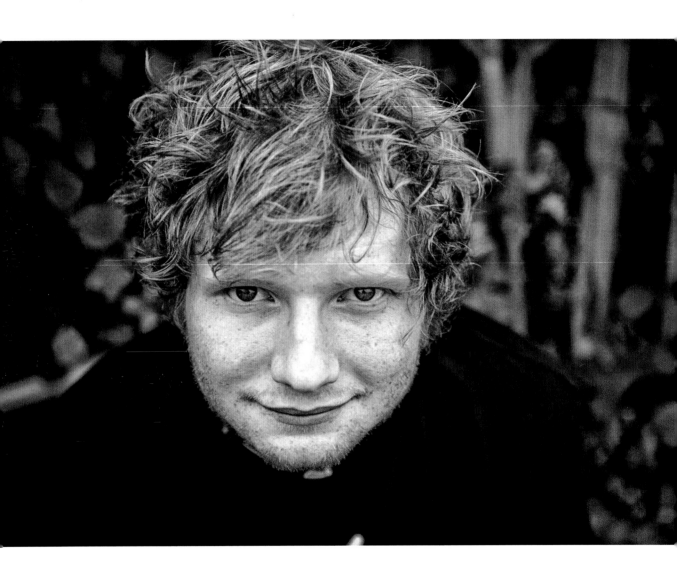

I had hoped that this would be my chance to shoot Ed for a full show, but the iTunes team wouldn't budge on that point. Because the show was streamed live and there were so many logistics involved for them, they could only allow me to shoot the first three songs from the pit.

As soon as Ed began, he had his loyal and excited crowd singing and clapping and hopping along to his songs. It's impossible not to get drawn in to his performance. At one moment Ed asked the crowd to hug the person next to them and everybody obliged. I had no one around me to hug so I popped out to the far edge of the pit where Patrick was sitting on a flight case with my gear and gave him a big hug. You just have to obey the master when he asks you to hug your neighbour, there is nothing more to it.

Even though I had to leave the pit after three songs, I did what I could to capture the essence of Ed on that night with my pictures. It wasn't too hard, because he did everything right from the start. Ed rapped, played, sang and hopped from one stage monitor to the other. His second song that night was "Drunk" and, remembering the beer kegs, I thought I'd try to get some nice wide shots at the right moment when the word "Drunk" appeared on the screen behind him.

I left the Roundhouse very content that evening. I still felt sad that I hadn't been able to get everything I wanted from a shoot with Ed, but I was getting close.

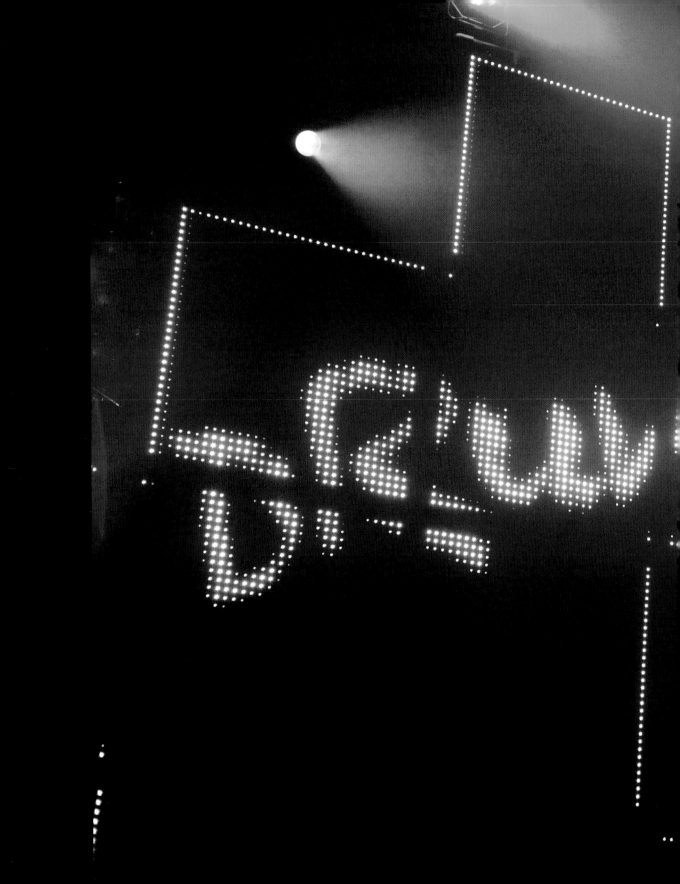

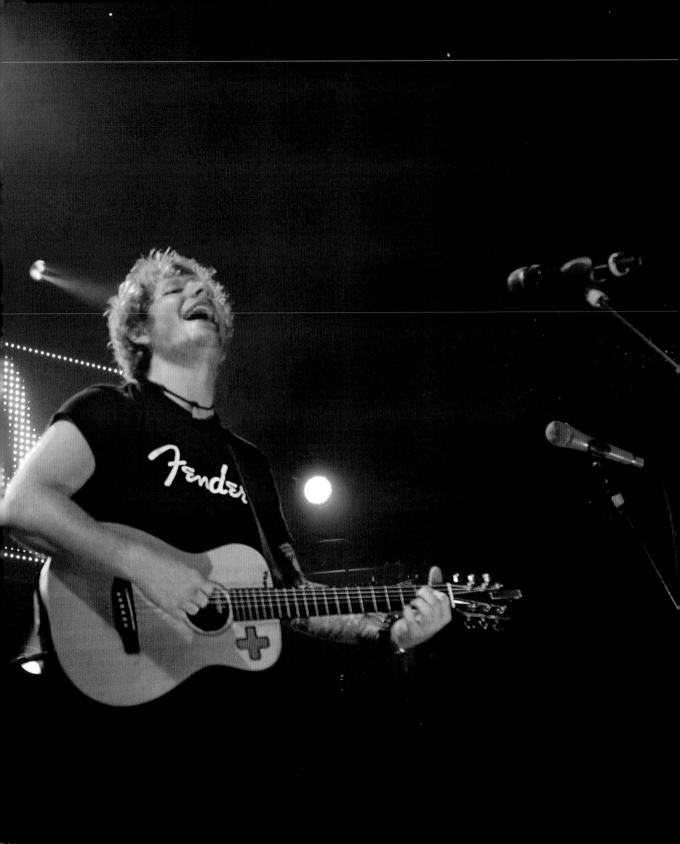

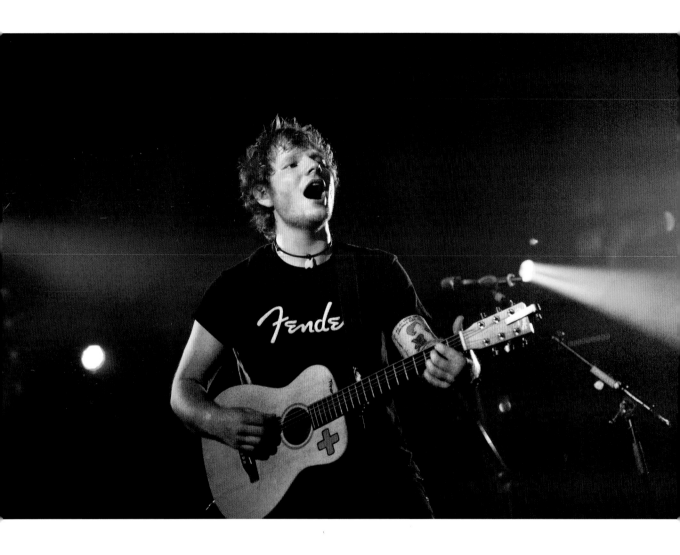

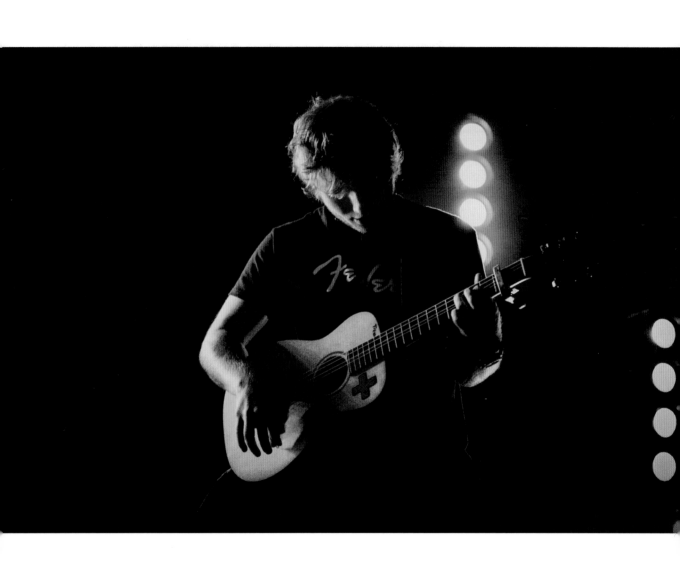

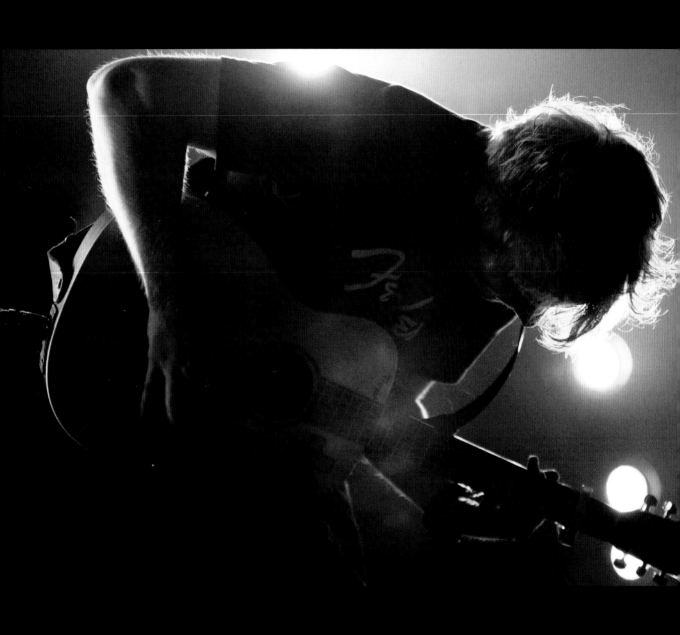

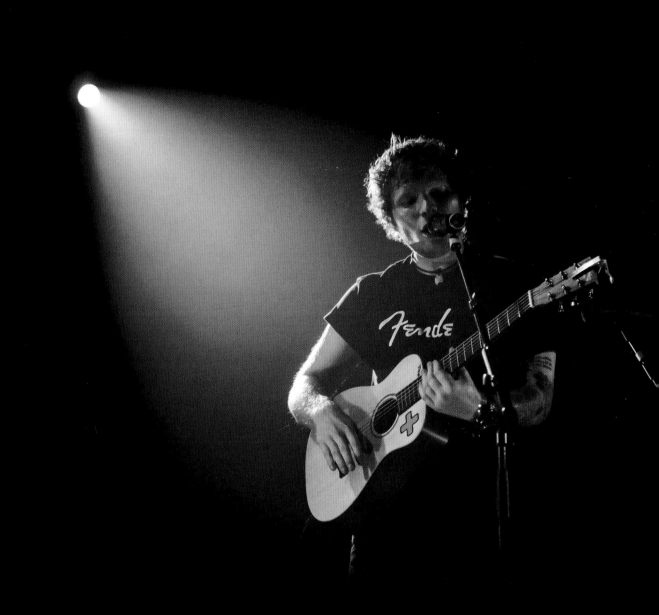

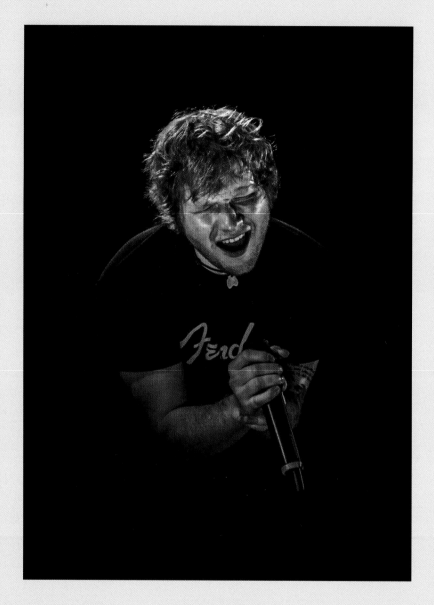

John Sheeran

I particularly like Christie's photos of Ed when she isolates him. You don't see the venue, the audience or the lights, the monitors or microphone stands. It's just Ed, here superbly lit, his features contorted with all that emotion, singing his heart out. I have met many people who have been equivocal about Ed and his music. They have later seen him live and then appreciate what he is all about. Ed was born to perform and is most at home playing to a live audience. It doesn't matter at all to him in front of how many. In the early days I saw him play to five or ten people, and he would give just as committed a performance.

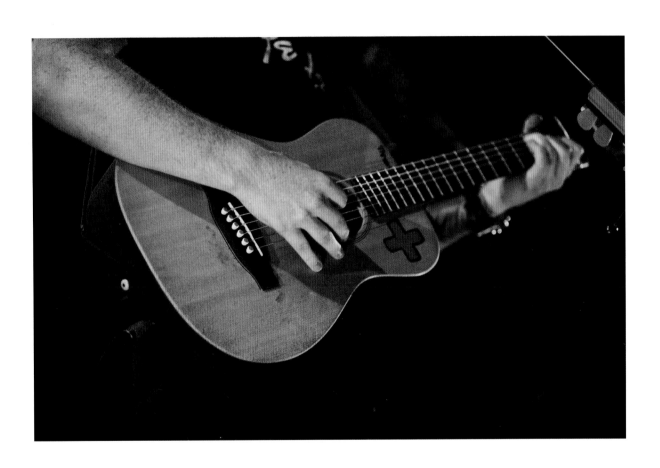

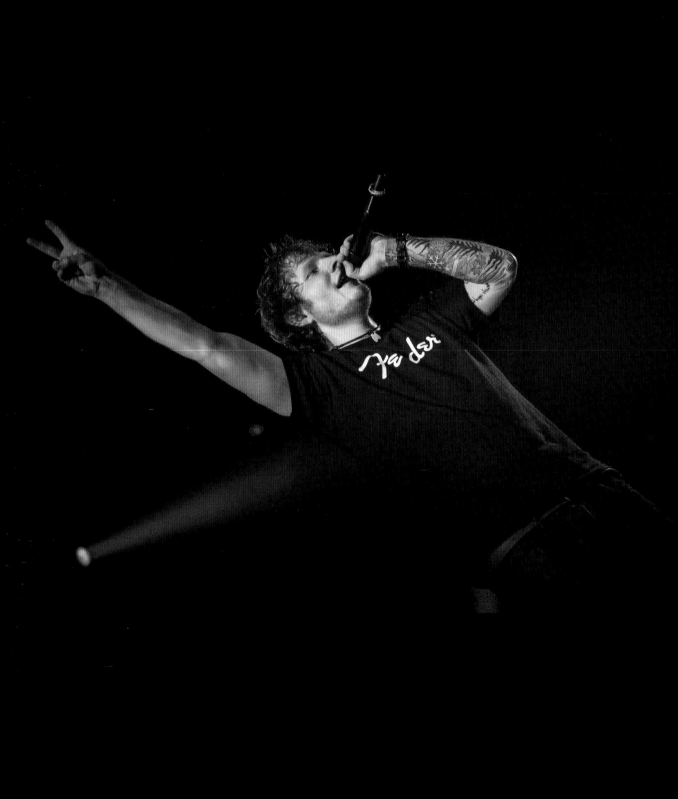

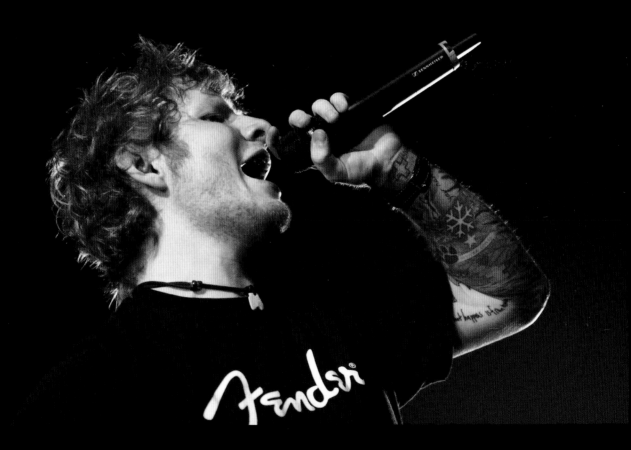

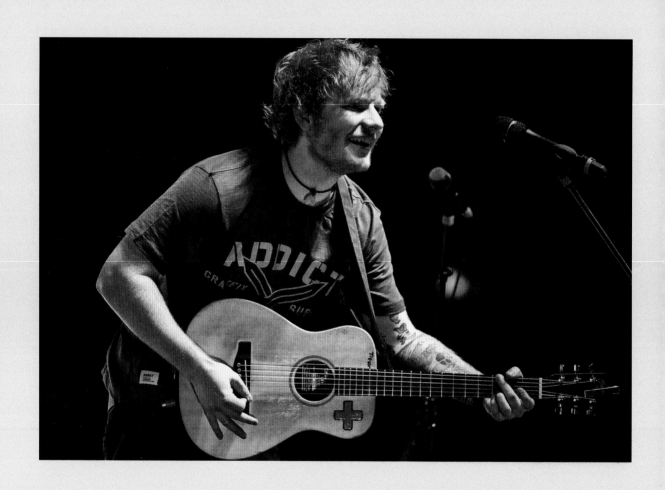

John Sheeran

Here are some shots that show just how much Ed enjoys himself onstage. It's obvious he's having fun. The smiles are broad and his eyes are lit up. We used to say to him when he was a boy that, if he could work in a job he loved, he'd have a great life. These photos prove it.

hammersmith apollo

— LONDON, 12 OCTOBER 2012 —

―――

THE PHOTO PASS DEBACLE

When you first start working with an artist you don't know what their story is going to be. When I began working with Ed I didn't know much about him, and it was only over time that I gradually learned and discovered more about him, mainly through my viewfinder. I most certainly didn't know where his story was going to go. The story started in 2008 when I first met this young and vibrant artist, who was quite professional from the get-go and had a strong will to succeed. He had a dream and he was chasing it with all that he had. And then something happened midway through the story that changed the narrative significantly. Four years later he was still a one-man band, but he no longer travelled clubs and set up his own gear with the help of his dad: he now had a crew, increasingly larger stages and increasingly larger crowds.

As a photographer, it is really important to allow yourself to be guided by the story wherever it takes you and not stick to preconceived ideas about where you think the story might or should go. That is one of the main reasons why when I shoot Ed I still see the Ed whom I first met a decade ago. I don't see a world-famous man through my lens; I see a guy who grew up in front of my lens. His surroundings have changed, and he is much more successful now, but the person I am capturing is still Ed – the same fiercely driven guy who is highly professional, has a love of his craft and a passion to succeed.

By October 2012 Ed's album + had really taken off, and venues like Shepherd's Bush Empire were too small. I was assigned to shoot Ed for press at London's Hammersmith Apollo, another legendary venue. It has a 5,000 capacity and pretty much anybody who's anybody in rock and pop history has played there since it opened in 1932. Just like Shepherd's Bush Empire it's a Grade II listed building.

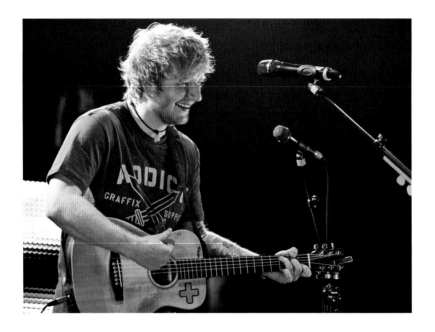

When I arrived at the box office that evening, the girl at the box office told me that there were no photographers allowed for Ed's show, so no photo passes. I stepped outside and contacted my assignment manager to get the details of the person who had approved my photo pass to her. What followed was a 20-minute string of phone calls to the promoter and PR people. The clock was ticking. Another photographer arrived at the box office and was given the same spiel – no photo passes for Ed's show. It might sound like a hassle, which it is, but it does happen more often than you would think. Sometimes for no reason at all you are lost in the chain of communications and your name just magically disappears from whatever press or guest list you were on, usually with very little time to spare.

I was about to throw in the towel and return back home with no pictures to show for my trouble, when I thought I would try one last call. I'm not the kind of person who likes to pull favours but I did have Ed's tour manager Mark

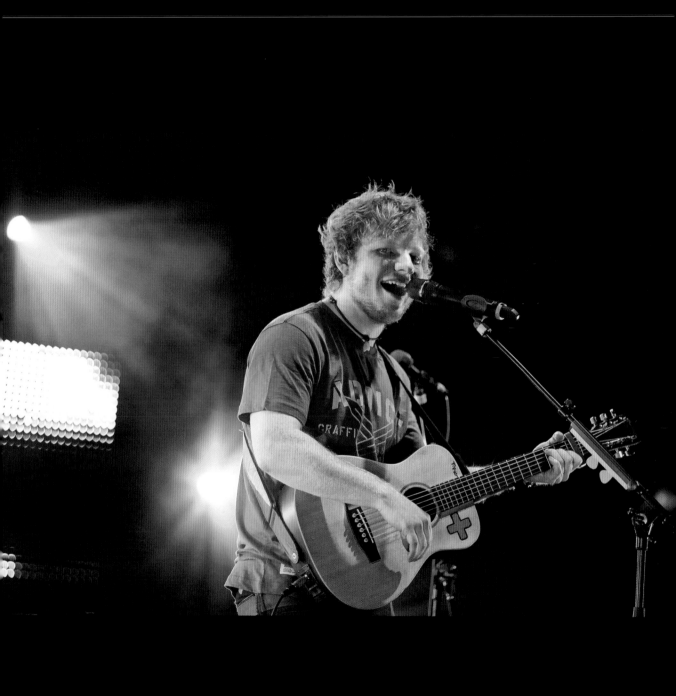

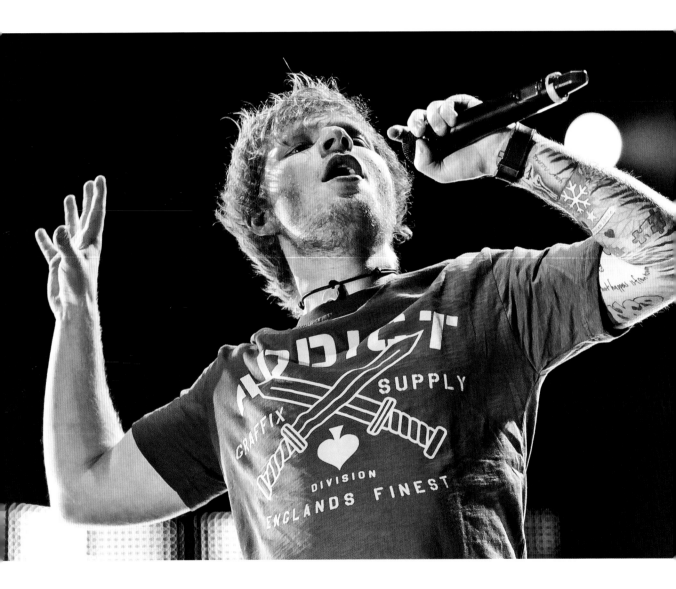

Friend's number on my mobile. Mark had been a big help a couple of weeks earlier at the Roundhouse, so I decided to give him a ring. I explained to Mark that I had arranged a photo pass earlier that week, but that there were none at the box office. Mark confirmed to me that no photo passes had been issued on the whole tour and that whoever had agreed to grant me a pass had made a mistake. There was a moment of silence and then a deep sigh left my mouth. Mark probably picked up on my despair, which prompted him to come and see me at the box office.

By now the support act had finished and it was only about 20 minutes till showtime. In my experience, this close to the gig there is very little hope of getting last-minute approval to shoot a show. Just ten minutes before showtime Mark popped up and handed me two photo passes. One for me and one for the other photographer. "Go on and get in," Mark mumbled, and he rushed off again into the crowd. I didn't even get the chance to say thank you. As is pretty much customary in live music, the tour manager escorts the artist to the stage every night. So, Mark had to really hurry to escort Ed to the stage a couple of minutes before the show, which just shows how he went out of his way to help me out. I salute you, Mark.

Just as we were ploughing through the crowd and arriving near the stage, Ed walked on. Perfect timing. It was that day at Hammersmith that I realized how much things had really changed for Ed – bigger venues, better lighting, larger crew, larger crowd – but when I peeked through my viewfinder it was still just Ed that I saw, with his guitar in hand and his loop pedal board at his feet. When I walked back to the Tube at Hammersmith to head home that night, I knew that things would never be as they were before – Ed was well on his way to becoming a megastar.

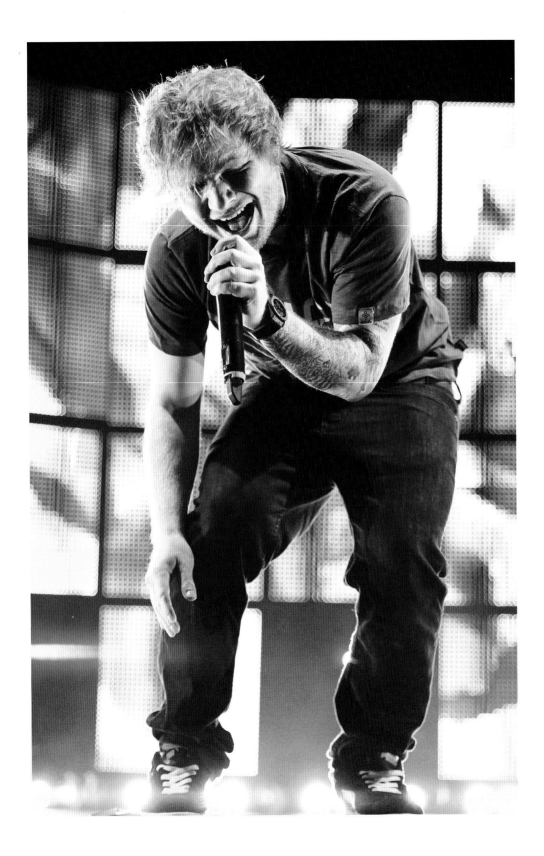

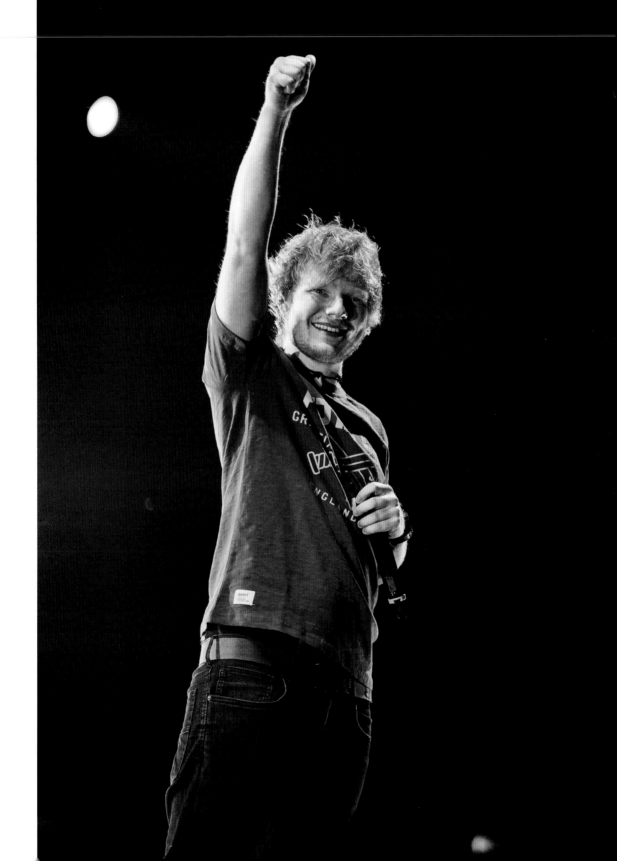

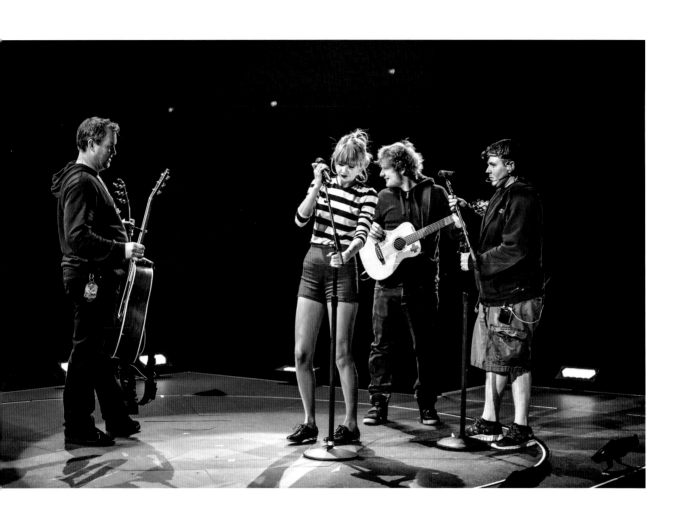

centurylink center

— OMAHA, NEBRASKA, 11–14 MARCH 2013 —

──

John Sheeran

Taylor Swift gave Ed his first big break in America by inviting him to be her support act for the US/Canada leg of The Red Tour in 2013. This gave Ed unprecedented experience of playing large arenas and multiple stadiums, and exposed him to a vast new audience and to the American media networks. Apart from learning a huge amount on tour and having a lot of fun, Ed also developed a strong, lasting friendship with Taylor, whom he admires greatly. This photo shows them in rehearsal at the CenturyLink Center Omaha, the first venue of the tour. Taylor adjusts her microphone stand while the stagehands wait either side. Behind her is a smiling and expectant Ed. You sense the anticipation as they are about to practise a duet of Taylor's single "Everything Has Changed".

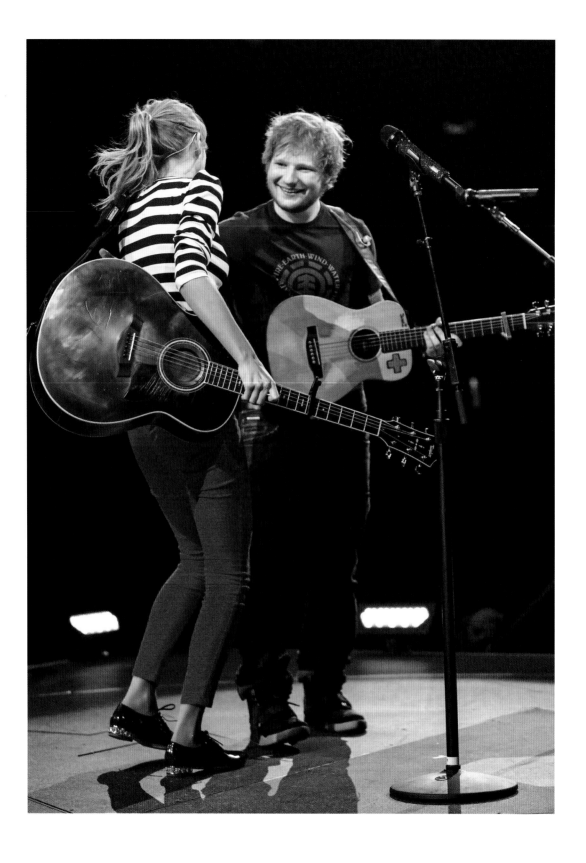

CONQUERING AMERICA

Back in 2013 I was commissioned by Taylor Swift's management to shoot the start of The Red Tour in Omaha, Nebraska. They flew me over to shoot most of the rehearsals and cover her shows in Omaha and St Louis, Missouri. Having me there at the beginning of her tour to capture every aspect of her performance gave them plenty of material for merchandise and promotion for the remainder of her two-year tour. So off I went to a very cold Omaha. It happens often when you are on tour that you run into familiar faces – crew members you have met on other tours; musicians you have seen with other bands. The touring world is a very small one indeed.

It took about three seconds to run into Galen Henson, the keyboard tech on The Red Tour. He's one of my oldest friends in this business; he used to be tour manager for Joe Satriani, one of my earliest clients. But there was one familiar face I was really excited to see. Ed was trying to break into the American market and what better way to do this than to perform as Taylor's support act on the US leg of the tour.

I remember the first night in St Louis, walking to the venue from our hotel. On our way we passed a group of singing teenage girls wearing Ed Sheeran T-shirts. I did a double-take because here we were on our way to a Taylor Swift concert and they were wearing Ed Sheeran T-shirts. It made me realize that America obviously had already started to embrace Ed Sheeran. I'd got to capture Ed during rehearsals of his duet with Taylor, "Everything Has Changed", which he would sing with Taylor in her show every night. On that first night in St Louis I had some time and Taylor's management was OK with it, so I got to shoot Ed's performance too.

The largest venue I'd captured Ed in had been Wembley Arena, at the Girl Guide Big Gig, but that was more like a mini-festival and he had sung only a couple of songs there. I'd shot his show at Hammersmith, where he had easily succeeded in getting the crowd to eat out of his hand in a matter of seconds. But these gigantic American sporting arenas, they were something else. And it wasn't as if he could go out and hug the audience or high-five the front row like I was used to seeing him do. I was really curious to see how he would work a crowd of this magnitude.

As soon as Ed appeared onstage the crowd responded with a passion and he never lost a minute of their attention. I only shot from the pit because of time constraints and stage logistics, that is why most of my images of that night are focused just on Ed, working his audience like a maestro. Midway through the shoot, I felt as if I was attending church and he was leading the gospel choir. Ed split the crowd in half, just like he had always done, and gave them each a part to sing. The crowd surrendered and shouted so loud it almost drowned out his voice. I've seen very few well-seasoned performers handle a crowd like he did that night.

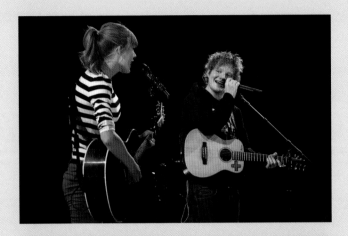

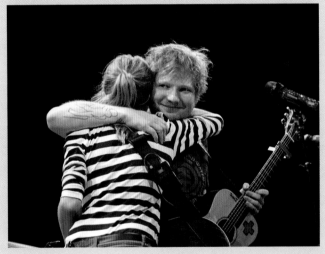

John Sheeran

These photos show Ed and Taylor performing the song in front of 17,000 people. They don't seem to have any nerves at all. The photos are from their first two performances in Omaha and already you can see the delight and infectious enthusiasm and affection they have for each other. They have since worked with each other professionally many times and remain protective and supportive, through the ups and downs of their lives. These photos are a wonderful record of when and where it all started.

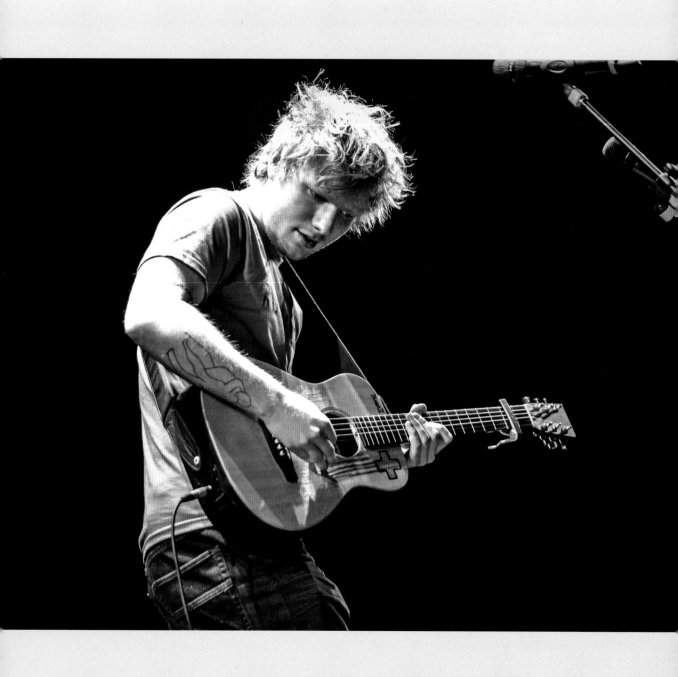

scottrade center

John Sheeran

This impressive sequence of photos was taken by Christie during Taylor Swift's The Red Tour in 2013 at the Scottrade Center, St Louis. They show close up the intense concentration and physicality of Ed's stage performance. He appears completely immersed in the music he is creating, as if possessed by it, and oblivious to the huge audience that surrounds him. Ed's battered Little Martin guitar takes further punishment as it is energetically plucked, strummed and beaten.

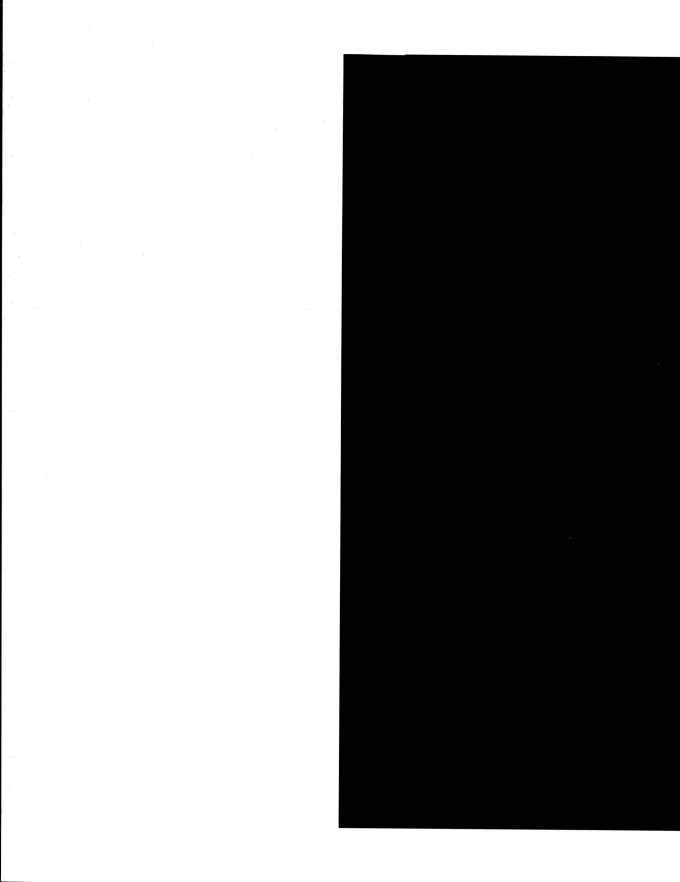

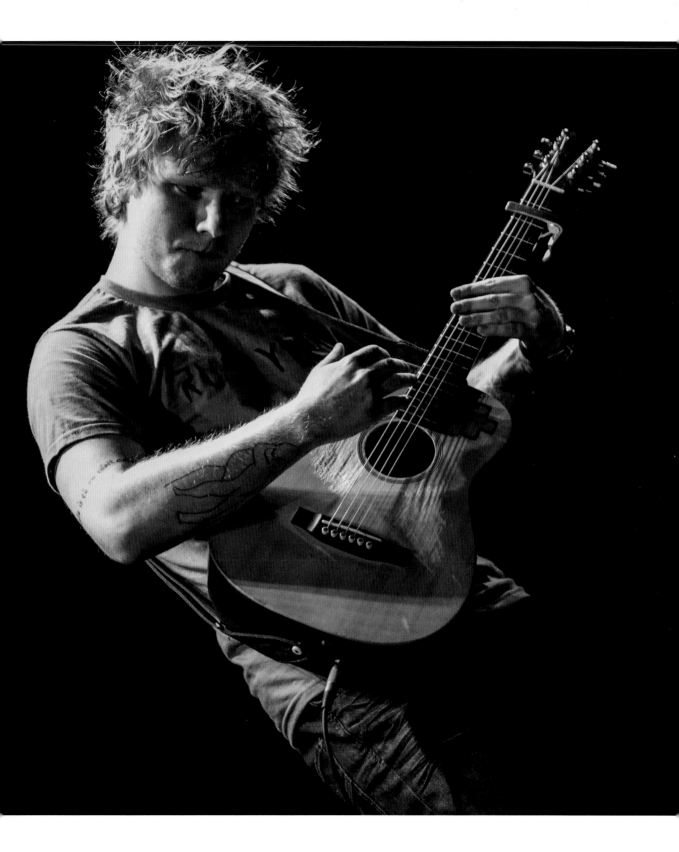

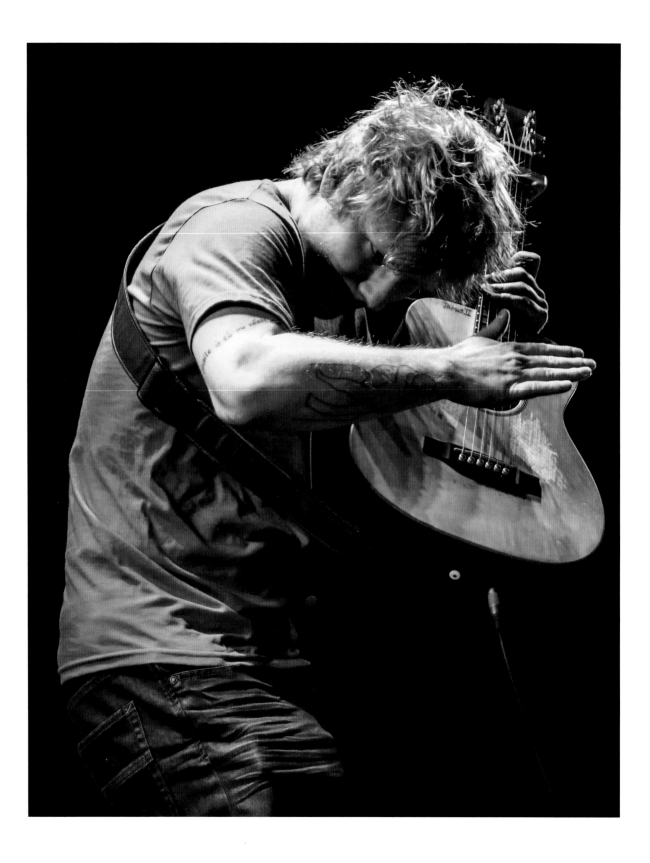

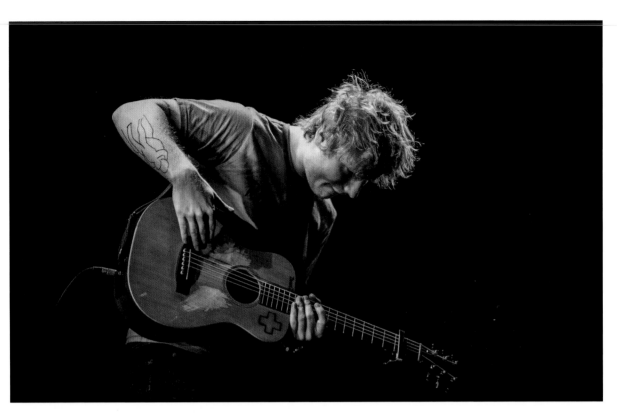

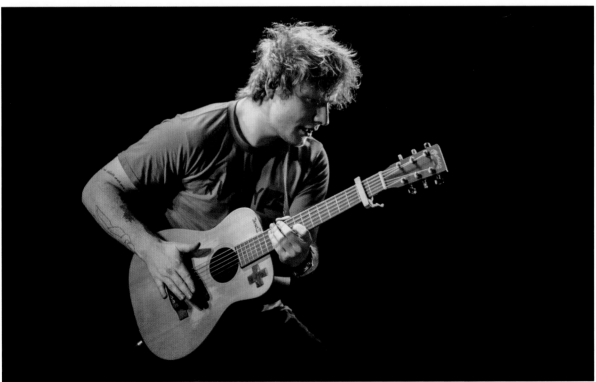

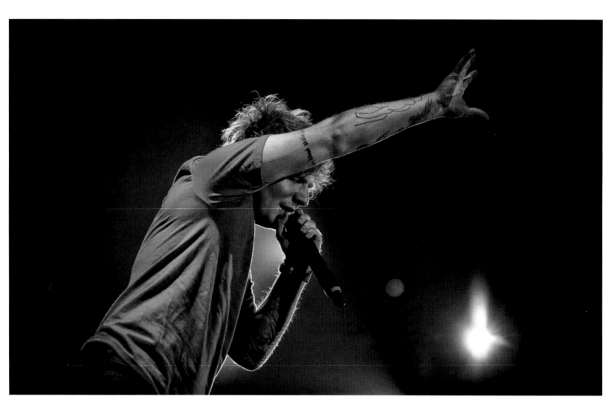
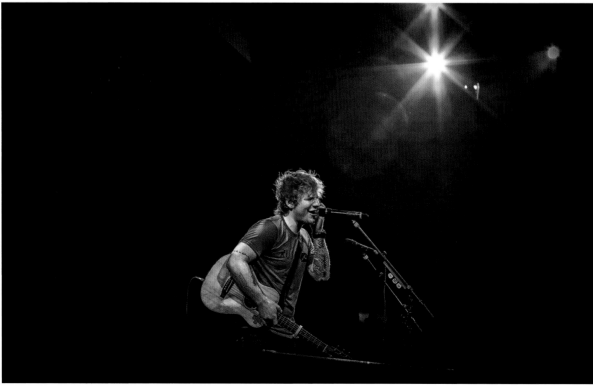

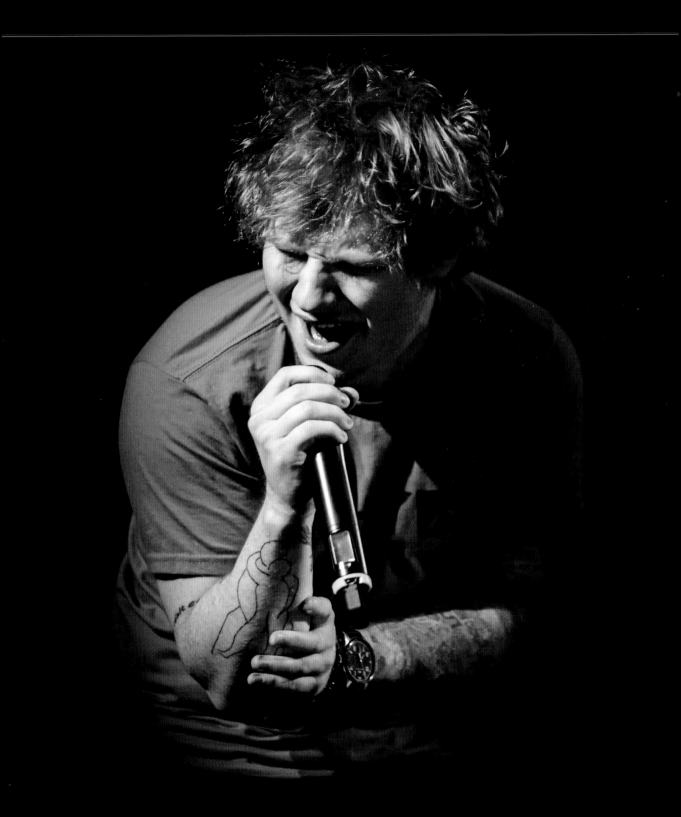

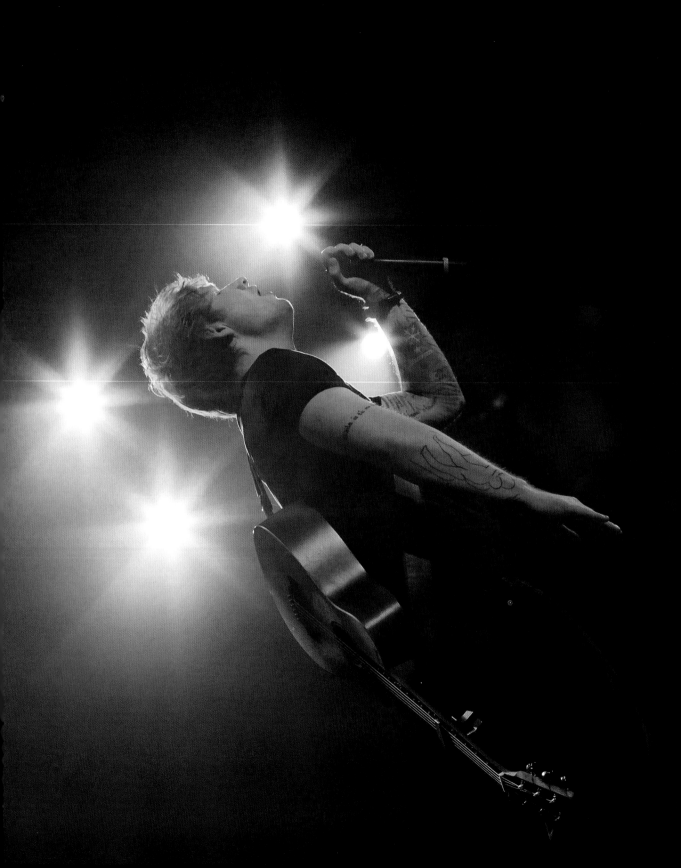

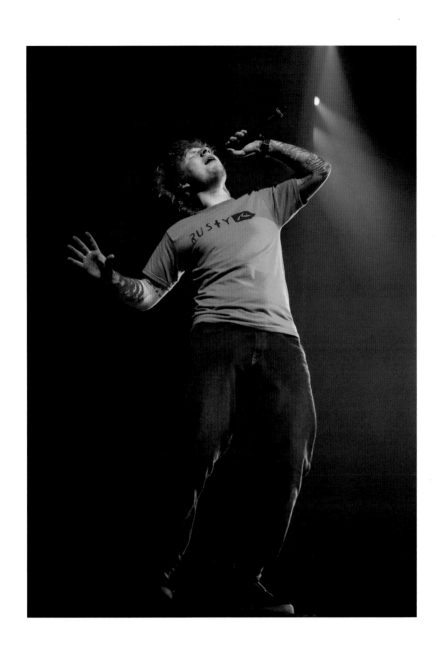

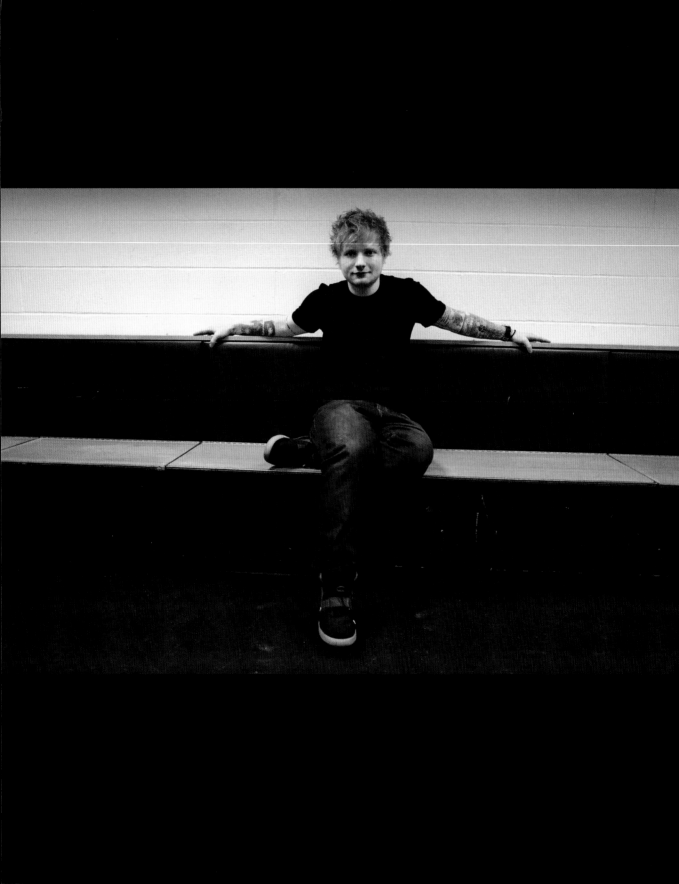

CHASING THE SCOOTER

As an artist, you have to allow yourself to be inspired by the works of others. I have towers of photo books by the great photography legends like Henri Cartier-Bresson, Diane Arbus and many others. In my kitchen, I used to have this picture by Nan Goldin – it was actually a postcard – *Misty and Jimmy Paulette in a Taxi, NYC*. I loved to just gaze at that picture while cooking dinner.

As I got into music photography, I regularly explored the works of music photographers who had set the path before me, like Baron Wolman, Jim Marshall and Terry O'Neill. Baron Wolman's Woodstock images, especially, just tickled my imagination. I was spellbound by those shots where you would see the artist in the front of the frame and behind them an endless sea of people. I had dreams I wanted to follow. I dreamed big and wanted to achieve big things. I too wanted to shoot a performance with a sea of people just like Baron Wolman had done at Woodstock. I too wanted to shoot unassuming portraits like Terry O'Neill's where you felt as if you were peeking into someone's private world. I too wanted to become one with my camera just like Jim Marshall used to be merged into his. It's these dreams that drive you to do better, to learn, to grow and constantly move the bar higher. Some of the goals I had ages ago seemed quite far-fetched and ridiculous back then, but I have achieved a lot of them and new goals have been set.

I can only imagine that when Ed first started out he probably had dreams, too. I have never asked him, but I am sure he must have had artists he looked up to and thought to himself, "I want to achieve that, too." You dream, and you have to dream big, but I'm sure neither of us could have imagined that only five years after Camden we would both be standing together in an enormous 20,000-seater American sports arena, Ed performing and me capturing it all.

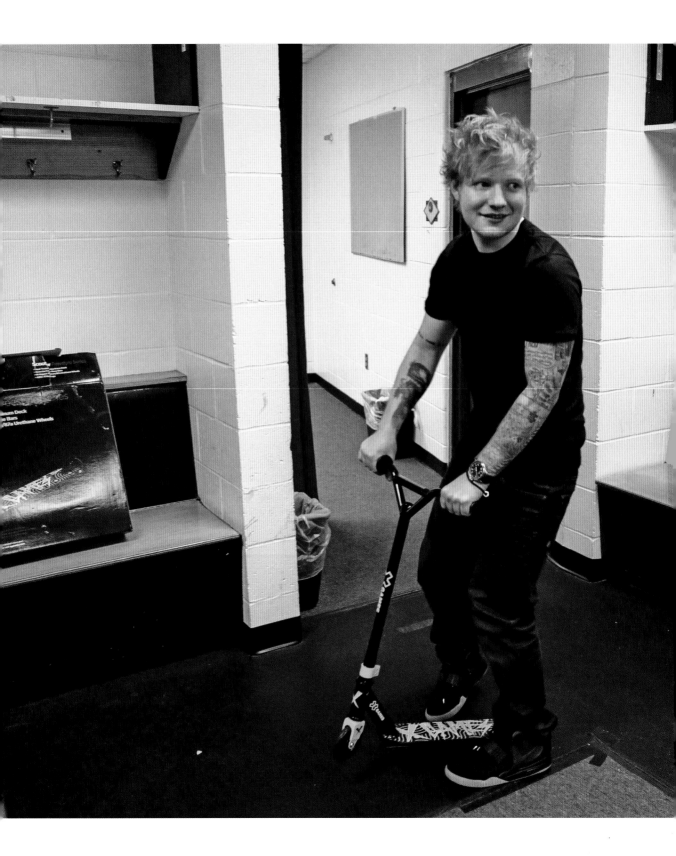

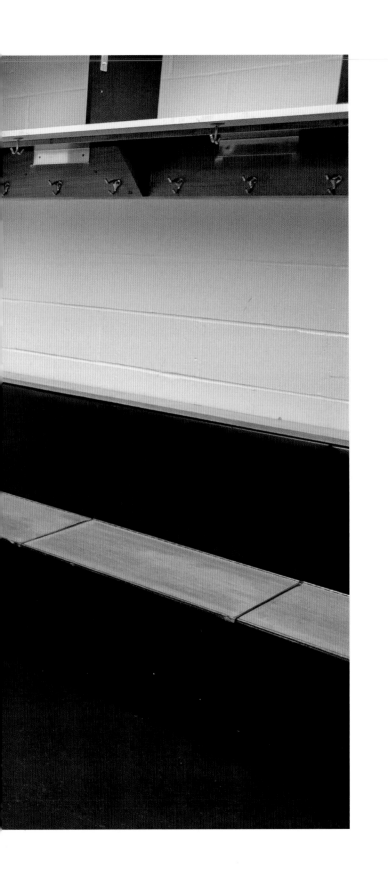

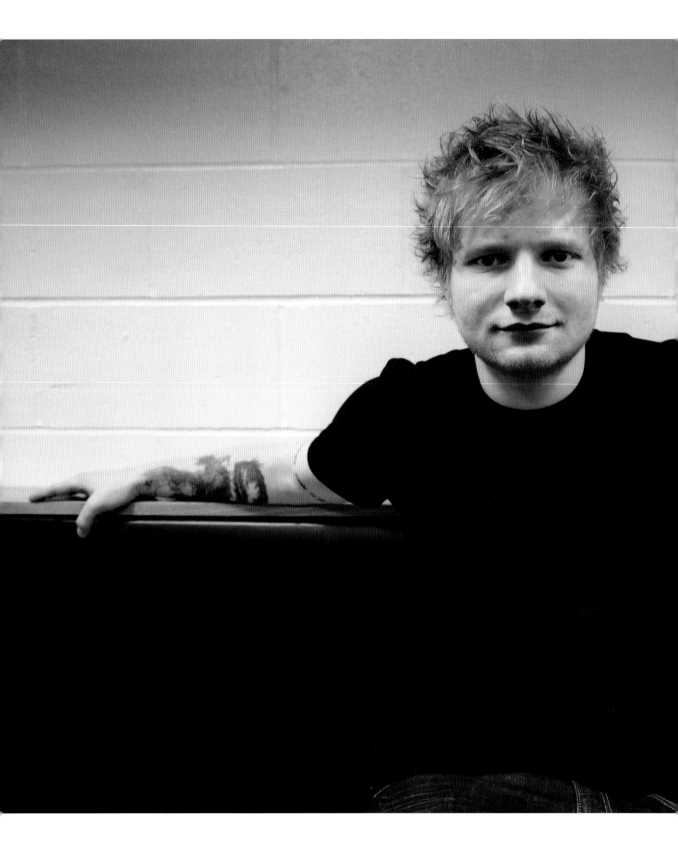

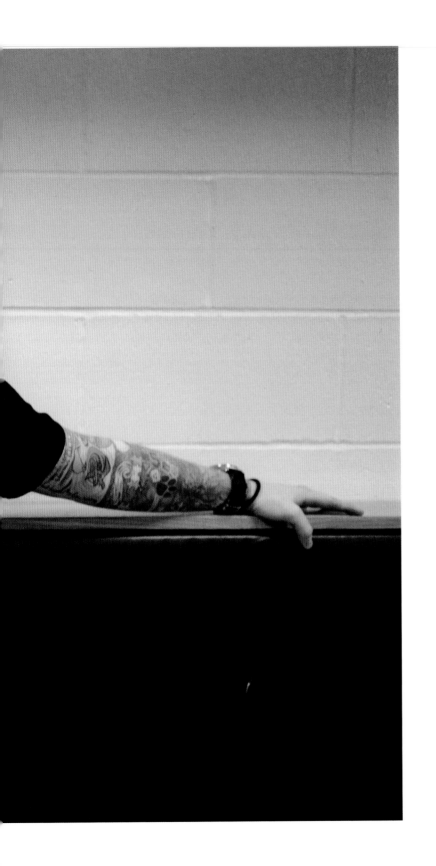

But here we were, doing just that. And, although it wasn't Woodstock, this one was very special to me. This was my opportunity to shoot Ed in an environment I hadn't shot him in before: backstage. There is just no comparison between a stack of beer kegs in front of a barbed wire fence outside the Roundhouse and the avenue-wide backstage corridors of an American arena.

As always, Ed's tour manager Mark was the one who helped me out, and a time and a place were arranged for a casual portrait shoot after the sound check on our last day on The Red Tour. I had suggested to Mark that he try to make sure that Ed would be wearing a plain unbranded T-shirt instead of a T-shirt with a company name or logo. Ed was getting to a level now where you just couldn't take chances. You never know what the pictures would end up being used for, and you always have to be careful that you don't run into any legal issues with trademarks and copyright when pictures are being used on a global platform. The morning of our shoot Mark and Ed popped into a local Walmart to buy some unbranded T-shirts. While passing through the checkout Ed had apparently clocked this step scooter, and he just had to have it. I have to admit that a step scooter is not such a bad idea to get around backstage in these huge American arenas. So, Ed bought the scooter – of course!

Later that afternoon, as soon as the sound check had been done, I went to meet up with Ed in his dressing room, which in this case was a gigantic room large enough for the St Louis Blues NHL ice hockey team, and Ed had it all to himself. When I walked in the room, Ed had just unpacked his brand-new scooter. I used the large space of the room to do a quick portrait of Ed sitting in his dressing room and then suggested we move to another location in the building. Since he was now a legit scooter owner he wasn't going to walk, obviously. He grabbed his scooter and, like the Road Runner, he flew past me into the corridor. Mark just grinned at me. "Good luck catching him, Christie." That's when the chase began. I ran behind Ed like a madwoman with my camera, trying to get a decent shot. He passed me a couple of times, whizzing through the corridors. And despite me trying my best to catch up with him, he was just too fast for me. This running around lasted for a good five to ten minutes. By now I had seen half of the bowels of the arena and I was pretty much running out of steam. Ed whizzed past me one more time and shouted, "Come on, Christie, catch me!" Really, Ed? Mark met

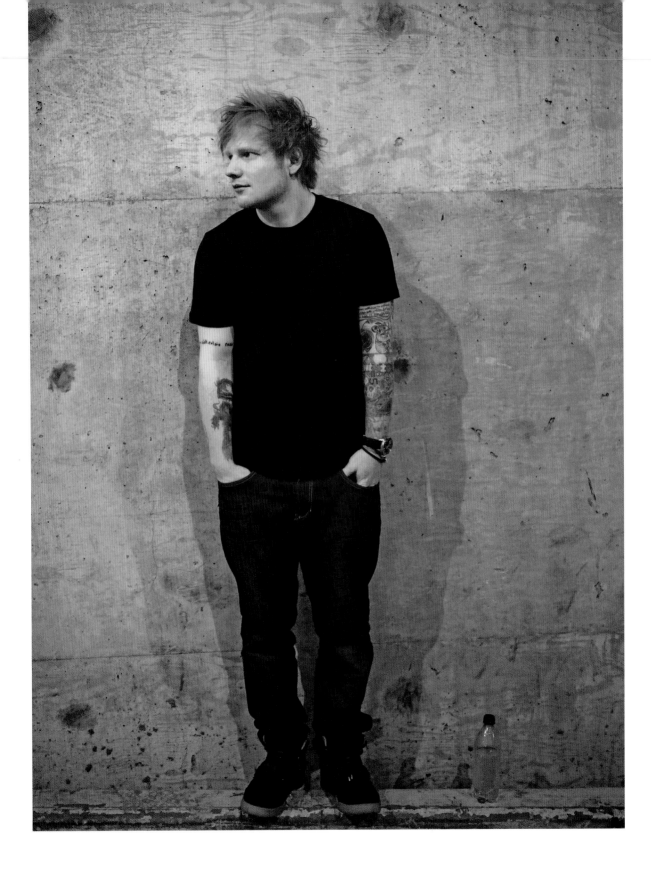

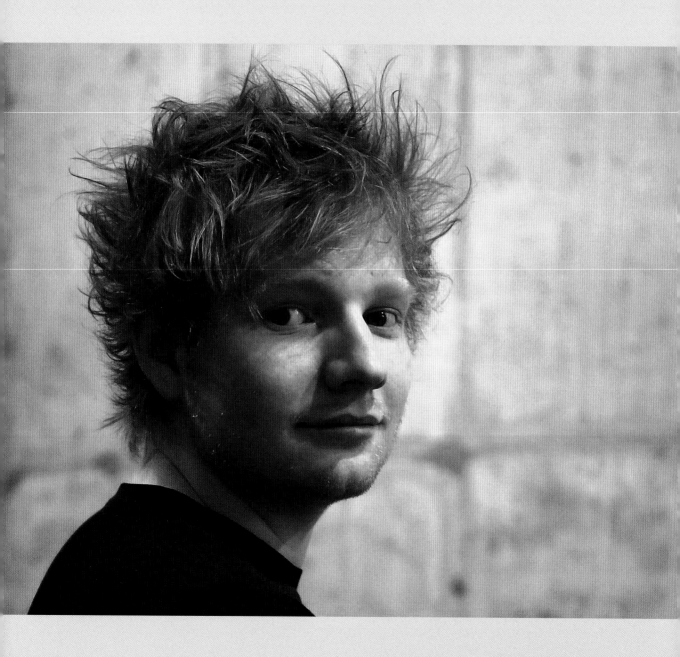

Christie Goodwin

When shooting a portrait session on location you really have to make do with what you have at hand, in this case a loading bay under an American arena. Just to stir things up a bit, I asked Ed to walk away from me and every time I called out his name he'd turn his head and look back at me. This is one of the shots from that sequence. It's very important to shoot in movement because the facial expression will be completely different from that in a still pose. Here, there is almost a wonder I can detect in Ed's eyes, the wonder whether I had got the shot or not.

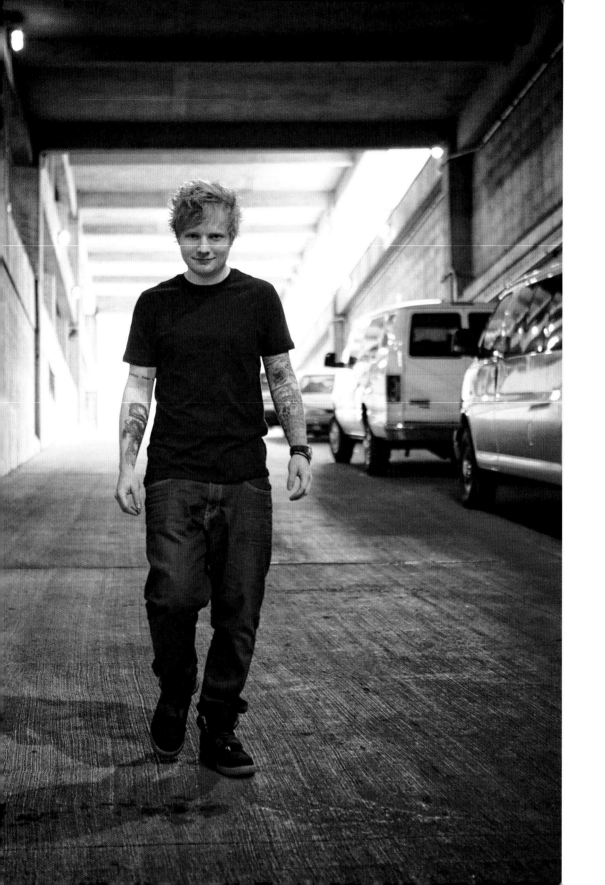

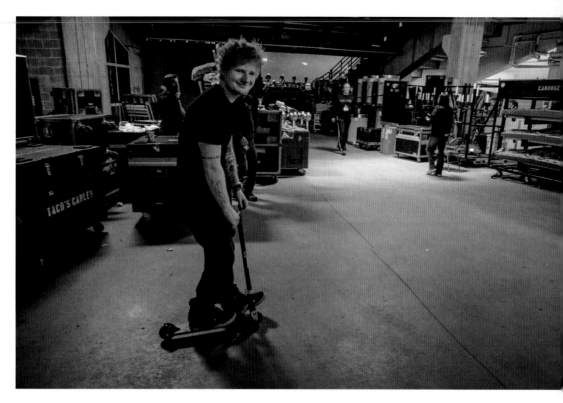

up with me somewhere along the way and said, "He's had his fun and now it's time for the shoot."

Ed got off his scooter, handed it to Mark, and we walked into the loading bay underneath the arena. All I needed was some plain walls, no frills, so the loading bay was the perfect setting. Ed is always very accommodating once I am alone with him. I give him very few directions, and everything just flows very smoothly and organically. There's a picture that came from this shoot of him looking to the right that has been used quite a lot by Ed and his label. I can disclose to you in strict confidence that that wasn't a posed picture. In fact, someone had just walked into the loading bay, passed behind me and walked to a door a bit further on. Ed just followed him with his eyes, and I took the shot. I got some close-ups, some full-length portraits, and to close off our little impromptu shoot I asked Ed to walk a couple of times up and down the ramp of the loading bay. That last one had probably less of a photographic purpose, but it felt good to make him work after making me run around like a lunatic earlier. We got through the whole shoot in under ten minutes. As soon as I said "It's a wrap", Ed grabbed his little scooter and disappeared as fast as he had arrived. But I got what I needed, and I have Mark Friend to thank for it. Again.

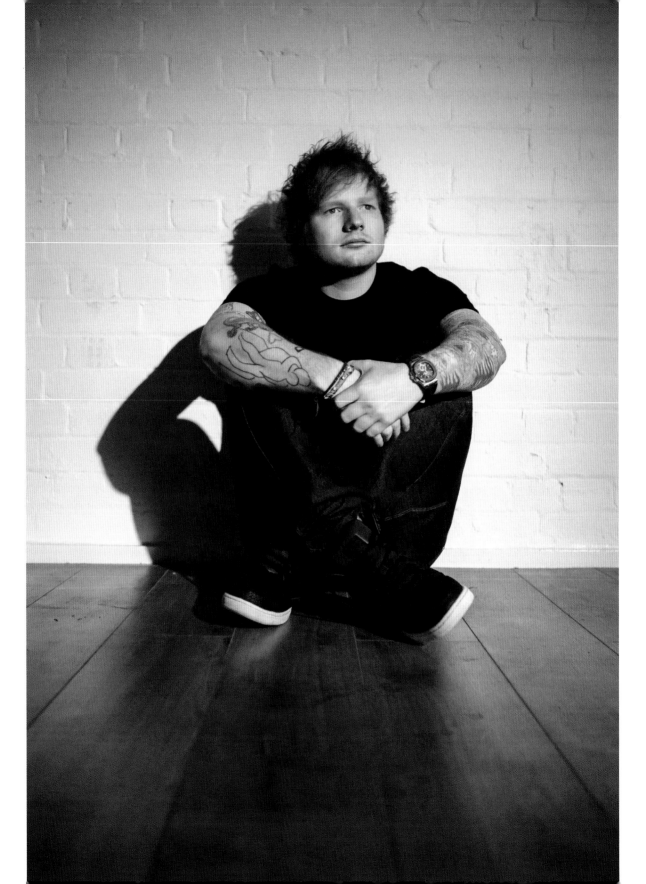

john henry's studios

— ISLINGTON, LONDON, 24 FEBRUARY 2014 —

STUDIO SHOOT

When this shoot came along I had already done some casual portrait shoots with Ed on location, always in tour environments. Personally, I don't like to shoot in a studio because I like to work with natural light. Photography is all about drawing with light, not fake light, but the light you have readily available, indoor or outdoor. In a studio environment, you rarely have the use of ambient light, and this makes the whole setting feel quite plastic, prefabricated, not natural.

Also, I'm an observer. That is how I photograph people. For me a story is more likely to unfold in a natural environment than in a studio, where your options become quite limited. It feels quite uninspiring to me. And because of that, a studio shoot can become quite awkward for both the subject who comes to the sitting and the photographer, as you are both in a place where neither of you really wants to be.

Every photographer has their own way of working in a studio. When I was still shooting fashion, we were not allowed to talk to the models. The models looked at the mood board and followed the poses that were laid out on the board. They knew what poses suited them best and how to show off the clothes. I just sat behind a camera and had to press the release button. Hence I got bored of it, really, really fast.

Some photographers like to have small talk with their subjects, some shout at the models, and some try to seduce them. I do all of the above, but in a casual, unforced way. I feel it is important that you adapt to the personality of who you are shooting to get the best out of them. You have to be an observer and perceive their mannerisms, the way they conduct themselves, the way they adjust themselves once you point your lens at them. And, most importantly, in all of that you have to allow them to be themselves.

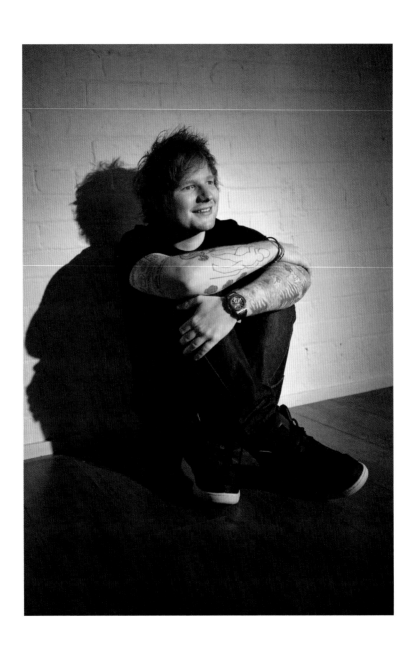

As often happens, this studio shoot with Ed was kind of a last-minute thing, and I had the freedom to choose the studio, just not a lot of time to do it in. I chose John Henry's studios in Islington, north London. I had worked there many times before and I liked it for this particular shoot because it's not a real photo studio complex; it's a rehearsal complex in old industrial buildings and warehouses. Bands come here to rehearse before going on tour. The energy there is all about music. There are six studios, and one of them works well as a photo studio. It has the added advantage that there is a central courtyard where you're spoiled for choice with the different brick walls, the outdoor staircases and cast iron railings, and the studio itself also has a wooden-floored roof terrace. It was February and in London, so the weather on the day could easily crush my hopes, but the plan was that, once I was done with the obligatory studio shots, I could take Ed outside and find more shots in a more natural setting.

We all met up that morning and it felt like a comforting reunion of old acquaintances. Ed, Stuart, the stylist Liberty and the record label Atlantic's marketing manager Callum, all pretty much arrived at the same time, and without wasting any time we just got on with it straight away. At first, I felt it was important that my manager and Ed's manager casually interact with Ed while I was shooting, so we could create some kind of normality. Quite often, it's the shots in between the poses that are the most interesting. So, as Ed was having casual chats with Patrick and Stuart, I could just observe and click. There was a green chair available, so I used that as a prop in some of the shots, which was a lucky coincidence as the new album was to be promoted with the colour green. We shot inside the studio for half an hour or so, but I just didn't feel very inspired. The place wasn't working for me, and I could feel Ed was getting bored as well.

As I'm friends with John Henry, the owner of the studios, I was allowed to go anywhere I wanted, even in their warehouses where they store all their rental touring equipment; it's packed with amps and instruments and flight cases. I talked it over with Ed and suggested we take a walk and leave everyone behind upstairs. Ed was game. Once we were outside the studio, the inspiration flowed. It was just the two of us, me and Ed, and some my favourite shots came out of that part of the shoot. I remember we were in the courtyard and I said to Ed,

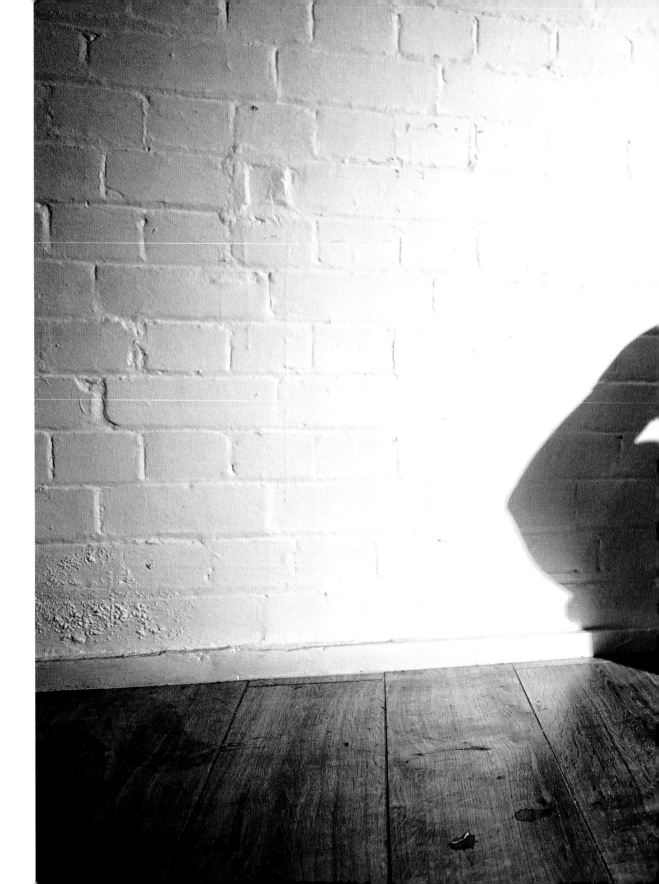

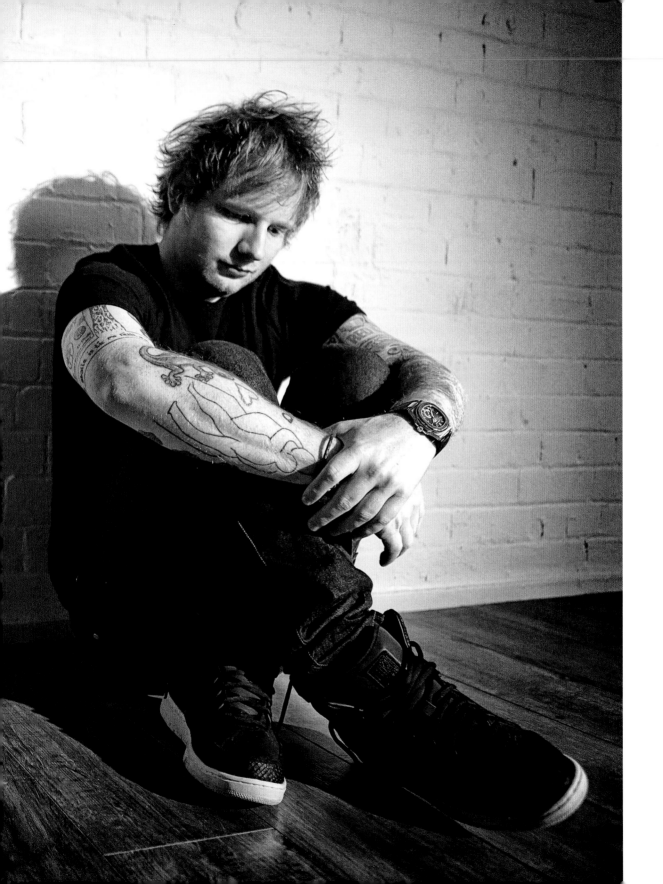

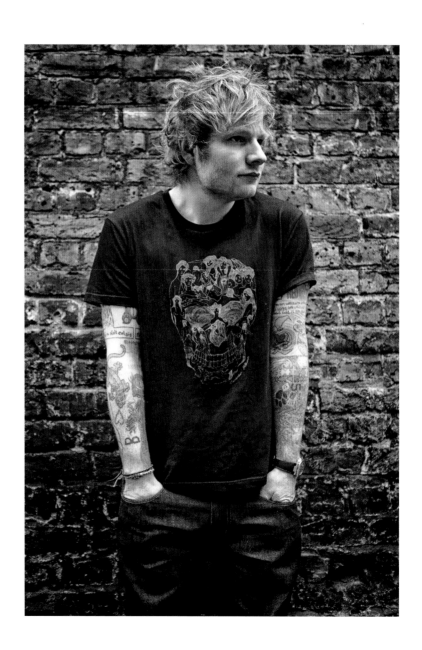

"Forget where you are and just pretend I'm not here. Just imagine you're standing in your backyard." He looked at me with a quizzical gaze, like he was thinking, What the hell is she talking about? "Remember, I'm not here!" I shouted excitedly. It made him giggle because it was hard not to notice me when my camera was so close up to his face.

We went into one of the warehouses, and being surrounded by all the familiar equipment and touring gear seemed to really put Ed at ease, as if he was in his natural habitat. Whatever I shot outside the confinement of the studio just worked from the first click. I work really fast. Musicians are very creative people and they are easily distracted, and very few enjoy a photoshoot. I always try to get it right from my first shot. I've noticed before that, no matter how many frames I shoot in any given setting, usually the first one is the one, spot on.

After about half an hour outside, no more than an hour in total, I thought we could call it a wrap. We returned to the studio. Ed joined Stuart, Liberty and Callum at the table and they had a quick business chat. I didn't put my camera down yet but used these candid moments to take some more close-ups of Ed just interacting with his people.

Some of my favourite close-ups come from that last sequence. I like it when I can just observe and capture the beauty I see. My drive is to capture and hold still beauty for eternity. Every picture that I have taken was taken from the heart, with a deep belief in what I captured.

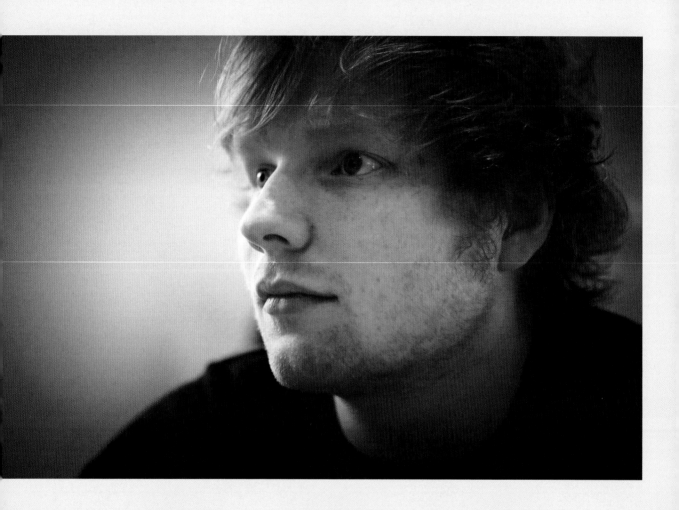

Christie Goodwin
After the photoshoot at John Henry's studios, Ed sat down with his people for an impromptu meeting and I never stopped shooting. I pulled up a chair and sat right next to Ed and waited for the right moments. Here, Ed is listening deeply to what Stuart has to say. I love the intensity in Ed's face in this one.

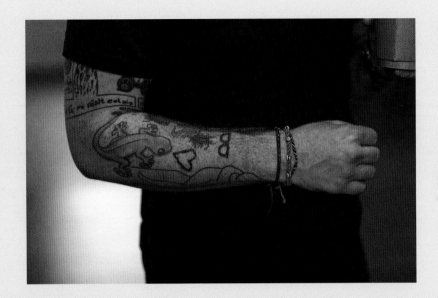

Christie Goodwin

I love tattoos. Since our very first shoot I have followed the development of Ed's tattoos with my camera. By 2014 his tattoos had really taken shape and were significant enough to merit a picture of their own.

Overleaf

John Sheeran

This is a behind-the-scenes shot from a photoshoot in a studio setting. There was a coffee break in the photography and Christie decided to take some casual shots of everyone. From left to right are Stuart Camp, Ed's manager; Callum Caulfield, marketing manager for Atlantic Records; Ed; Patrick Cusse, Christie's partner and manager, and Liberty Shaw, Ed's stylist. The body language, gestures and expressions tell us a story. You sense Ed is proposing something to Stuart, who looks questioning, slightly disbelieving. He has had to deal with years of Ed coming up with crazily ambitious ideas, some of which have worked, others of which Stuart has managed to neutralize. Callum seems to be on Ed's side and is supportive. Liberty is probably thinking "Oh no, not another mad idea being floated"; and Patrick is enjoying the banter and awaiting Stuart's retort to Ed.

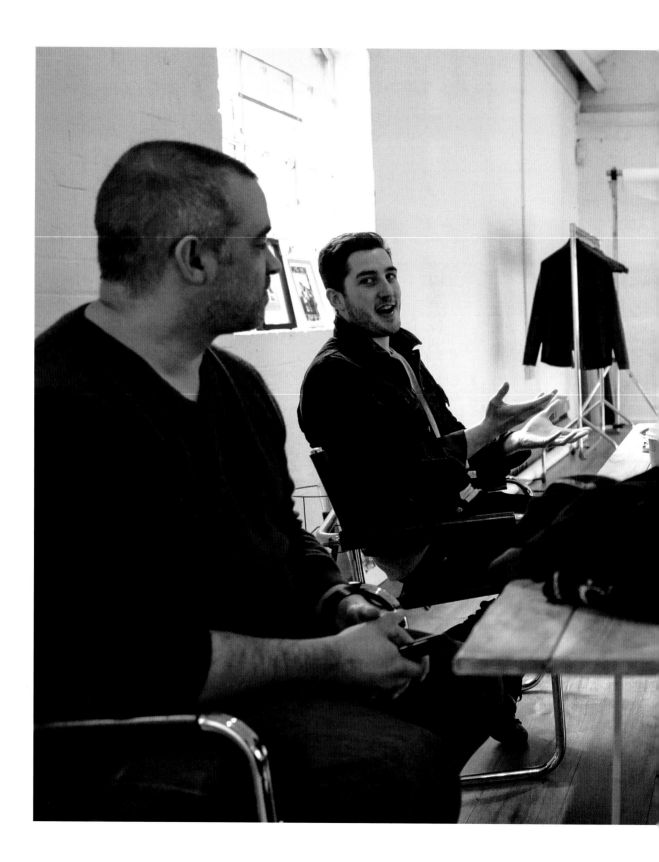

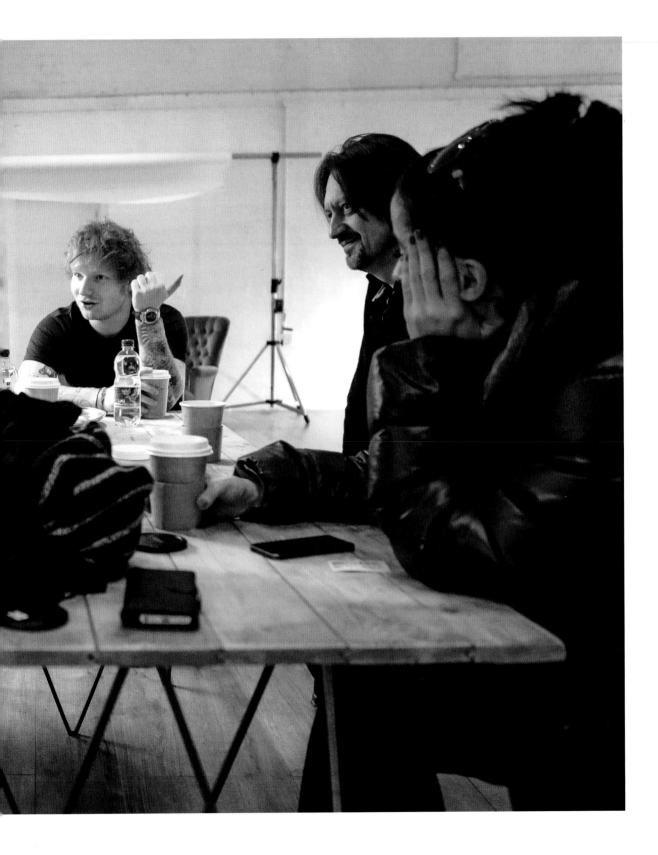

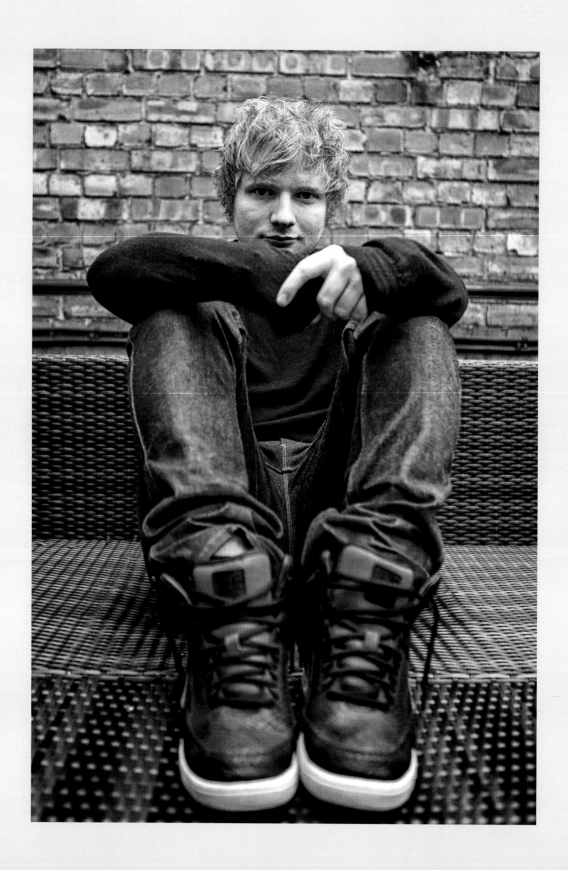

Christie Goodwin

This is one of the first pictures I took once we had left the confinement of the studio at John Henry's. Everything just became so much more relaxed and spontaneous. Even just Ed sitting down like this has a much more relaxed feel than the other pictures shot inside the studio.

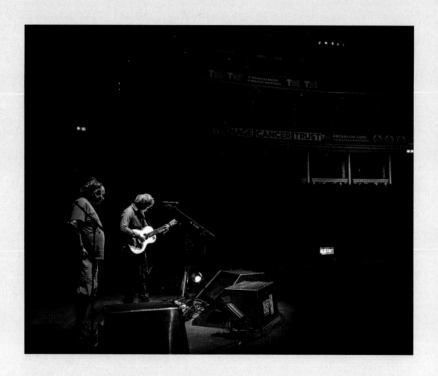

John Sheeran

Here Ed is doing a sound check in the Royal Albert Hall in 2014, a couple of hours before performing in aid of the Teenage Cancer Trust. Alongside him is his highly experienced guitar tech, Trevor Dawkins, who, like many of Ed's crew, has been with him for many years. Ed has his guitars specially tuned for each song, so Trev has a rack of them tuned and ready immediately behind stage. For every gig there is a non-stop Ed–Trev relay of guitars, and there is often the need to replace a guitar with broken strings, which is done so smoothly by Trev that Ed never has to interrupt his flow.

teenage cancer trust

ROYAL ALBERT HALL DEBUT

Whenever people hear that I work with Ed Sheeran, there is always that split second when they stop breathing, their eyes widen and occasionally the jaw drops. And I don't really get it. I'm like a primate in that weird celebrity culture world I'm often dropped in. I'm just completely oblivious to it all, so getting such a reaction from people is always a strange experience. On top of that, I find the fascination people have with celebrities troubling.

I remember a scary experience during a shoot with One Direction in Dallas. During their gig the boys had stopped their show in front of 20,000 people and introduced me onstage so I could get a posed group shot mid-concert. Later in the show the boys appeared on a smaller stage in the middle of the venue. They were transported there via a secret tunnel, but I had to make my way through the crowd. So, quite innocently, I started walking into the crowd and one girl screamed, "You're One Direction's photographer!" And literally in a matter of seconds there were hundreds of girls on top of me all trying to get a selfie with me, and I have never felt so scared in my life. If it hadn't been for Harry's security guy who came to my rescue, I probably would have suffocated right there that day. What a selfie that would have made, huh?

What people tend to forget is that this is my job and, for what it is worth, it's just a regular job to me. I have a job to do and I will always try to do it to the best of my abilities, whether it's a portrait of the guy next door or shooting the world's biggest chart-topping sensations. Same difference to me. But the general public is blinded by the magical bubble musicians and bands are shrouded in.

Don't get me wrong, I am appreciative for the opportunities I get and one of my favourite parts to my job is being one of the in-house photographers at the

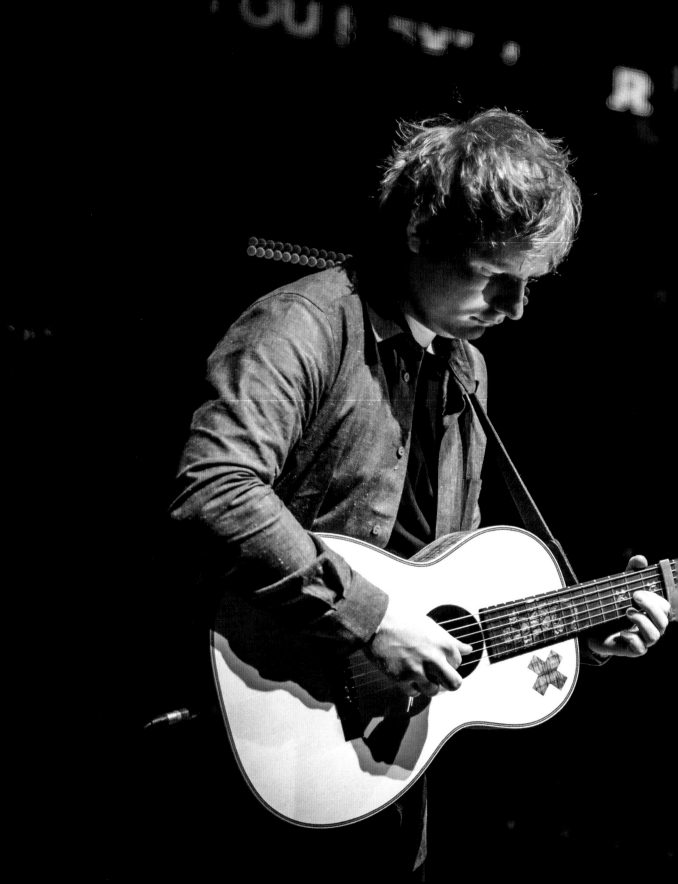

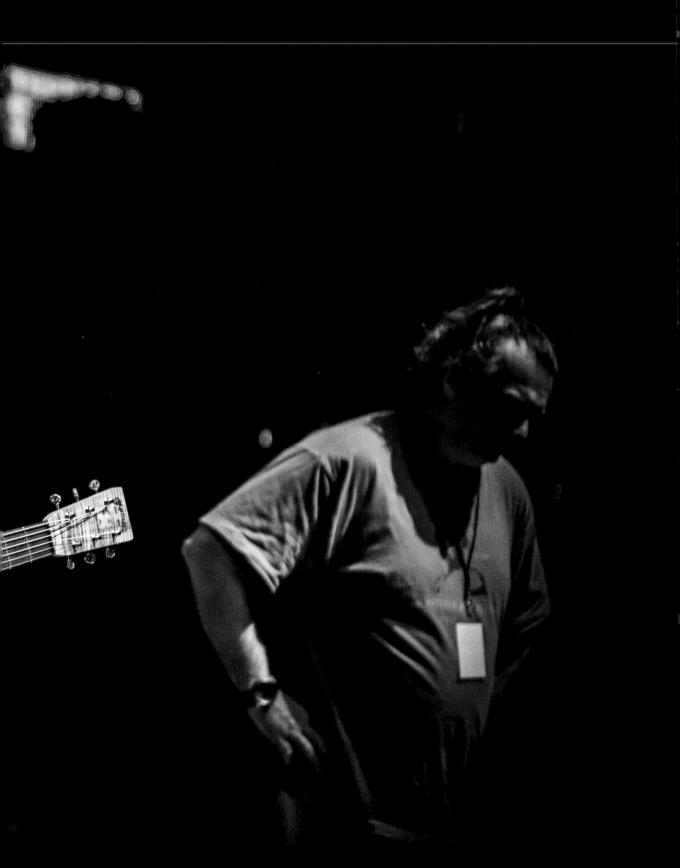

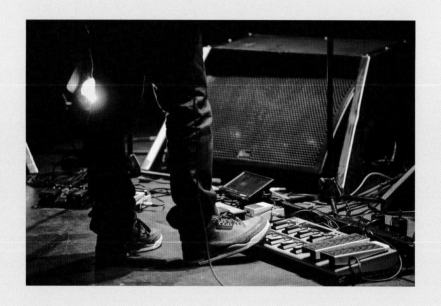

John Sheeran

Ed bought his first electric guitar wah-wah pedal with the proceeds from busking for a day in Galway, Ireland, aged 13. He later progressed to a Boss loop station, which, in the absence of a band, he used to record and layer multiple sounds live on stage. The more complex his layering became, the greater the need for something more multifaceted. This photograph shows Ed's use of the Chewie Monsta, a unique loop station that was custom-built for his sound. It enables him to create a sophisticated layered mix of guitar, vocal and percussive sounds.

Royal Albert Hall. This concert hall was opened by Queen Victoria in 1871 and it's probably one of the most famous venues in the world. If you wander around the corridors, you'll see framed prints of photos taken at the hall of the world's biggest all-time legends. Royalty witnessed shows there ... Nelson Mandela ... Princess Diana as well. Frank Sinatra sang there. Muhammad Ali boxed there. You get the idea. The Albert Hall has a huge archive documenting as much of its history as possible, and that's why I regularly get hired to shoot their shows. It is probably my favourite venue in the whole wide world to shoot at.

One of the Albert Hall's recurring major events is the annual Teenage Cancer Trust charity concert series. On 24 March 2014 I was asked to cover Ed's debut show there. Debuts are something the Albert Hall is always eager to document, so I was happy to oblige. As I arrived at the stage door, it was immediately obvious that Ed was in the building. There was a long string of girls huddled on the pavement all around the building, hours before the doors were to open. Quite an unusual sight there in my experience.

The people running the Royal Albert Hall always like to get as much as they can get from the event, and thanks to my relationship with Ed and his entourage I had access to shoot the sound check, some behind-the-scenes stuff, and the meet and greet. Mark Friend, Ed's tour manager, had also arranged with Ed that I could have a quick casual session in his dressing room after the meet and greet. It was bound to be an exciting day for me and my little ol' camera.

Downstairs in the backstage area, I could hear Ed playing. I walked onstage and saw Ed and his loyal guitar tech, Trevor, sound-checking. It's usually quite dark during the sound check. Everybody is doing their own thing; it usually isn't anything like what you see later in the evening. Quite often the light engineer is still testing and fine-tuning the lights, and not necessarily shining them on Ed. A couple of modest lights were lit to enable Ed to find his way to his gear, and I made full use of them. As I said before, work with what you get, right?

Backstage, the Teenage Cancer Trust team was busy escorting young people who were fighting cancer into the green room where the meet and greet would take place. There were snacks and beverages spread out on the tables. At the back of the room there was a branding board where Ed would be meeting his fans. The Teenage Cancer Trust's patron, Roger Daltrey of classic rock band The Who, walked in to check on the fans. Daltrey is the driving force at the annual Royal Albert Hall shows, bringing together top artists and comedians from around the world and raising millions to help support young people with cancer. Since 2000, and at the time of printing, the concerts at the Royal Albert Hall have raised over £24 million ($34 million).

The young people were all eagerly awaiting Ed's arrival. As soon as he walked in, they flocked around him and he patiently took the time to meet each one of them and happily posed for the obligatory selfies. His friend Passenger, who was the support act that night, also joined the meet and greet. After the meet and greet the fans were escorted out of the green room and Ed turned his attention to the journalists for the interviews.

Shortly after, I popped into Ed's dressing room with my camera. He looked up and said, "All right, where do you want me?" I told Ed to make himself comfortable. He looked up at me and said, "I feel most comfortable when I'm holding my guitar." "Then you must hold your guitar," I replied. It felt quaintly familiar how just by holding his guitar he would feel so much more comfortable, because I too only feel comfortable when I am hiding behind my camera. I pointed out to Ed that we were odd, both feeling so much more comfortable hiding behind our instruments, and he smiled and replied, "We understand each other." There's a mutual respect for each other's boundaries, and that will always deliver the best results. A photographer doesn't really belong in the artist's space, whether that be in their dressing room or onstage. But sometimes the job requires you to pop into their space to get the shot, and I always try to do this with humility and without disturbing or changing that space too much. I try to be mindful of the privilege I have and not to overstep boundaries.

There's always a certain easiness shooting Ed. We don't talk much. I let him get on with what he's doing and he lets me get on with what I am doing. I like it just like that. It took me no more than ten minutes in his dressing room to get exactly what I needed. Just me and Ed, just shooting him in his natural surroundings, with the ambient light available. When I had finished shooting we hugged, I thanked him, and I left.

As I walked out of the dressing room I bumped into Ed's parents, John and Imogen. It had been six or so years since we last met, back when Ed was working

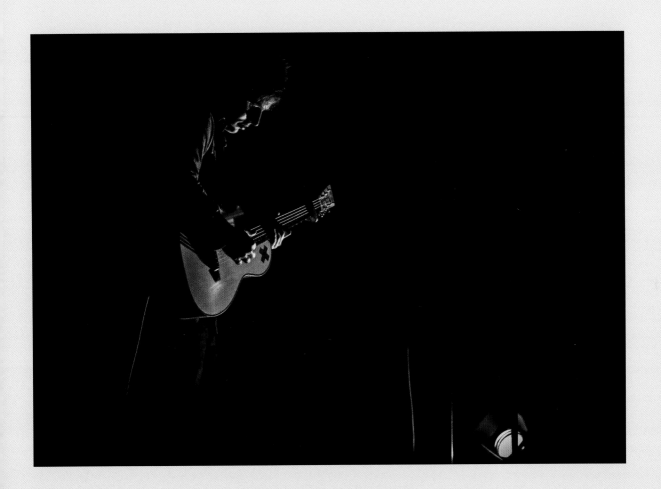

Christie Goodwin

During a sound check there usually isn't a lot of light available, but that never stops me from capturing those moments. This picture taken at the Royal Albert Hall shows exactly how dark it can be. You can see the light source, which reflects a modest amount of light onto Ed and his guitar. Especially in this shot you can feel the intense relationship between Ed and his instrument. I love these kinds of moments, as they reflect perfectly what a sound check is all about.

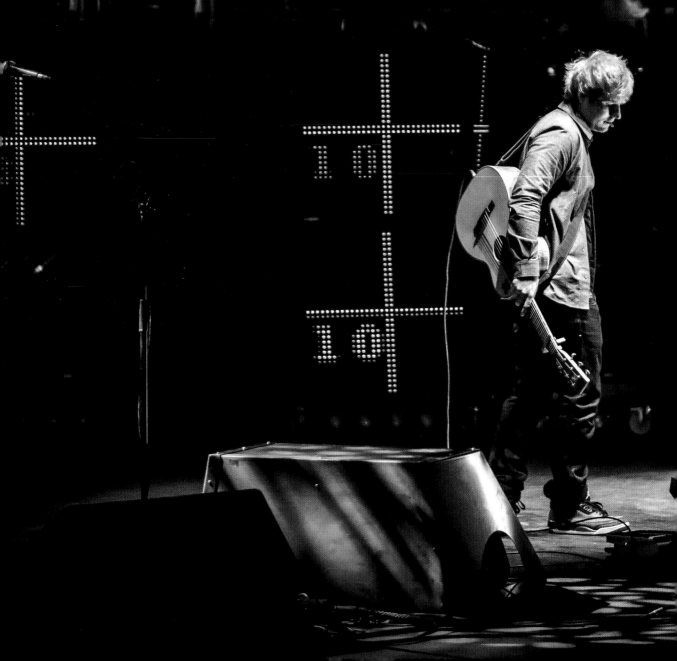

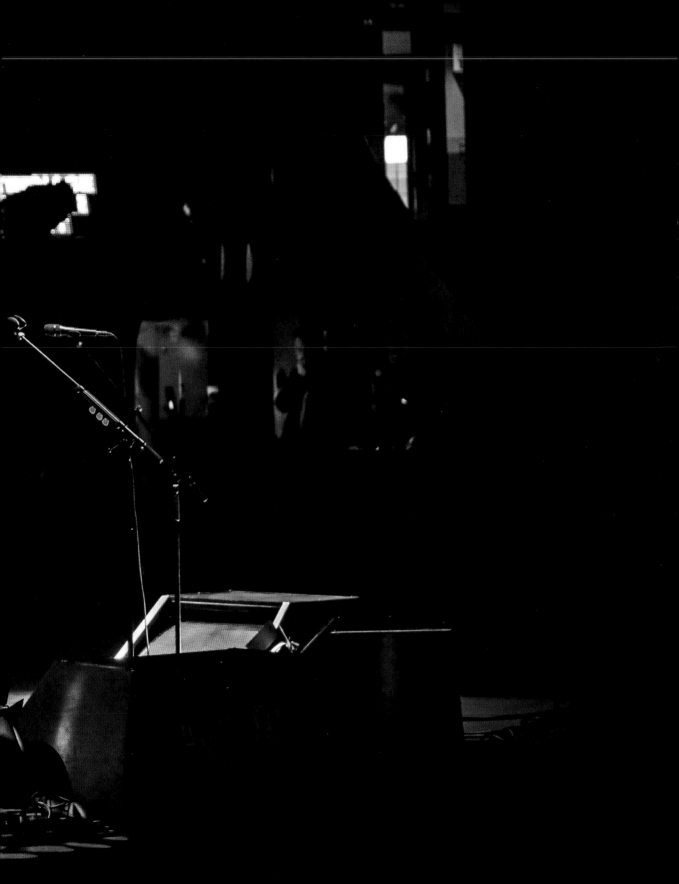

Christie Goodwin

This is one of those moments that I call "lucky shots". This was at the end of Ed's sound check at the Royal Albert Hall and people were packing things up. I was behind the screens walking off stage when I noticed a very poised Ed standing there looking into the darkness and I knew I had no time to waste. It's one of those moments that probably lasts two seconds and then the moment is gone. I had no time to run in front of the screen, so I chose to capture it through the screens. You will notice the lines from the screen throughout the picture. Still, I got the moment and that is all that matters.

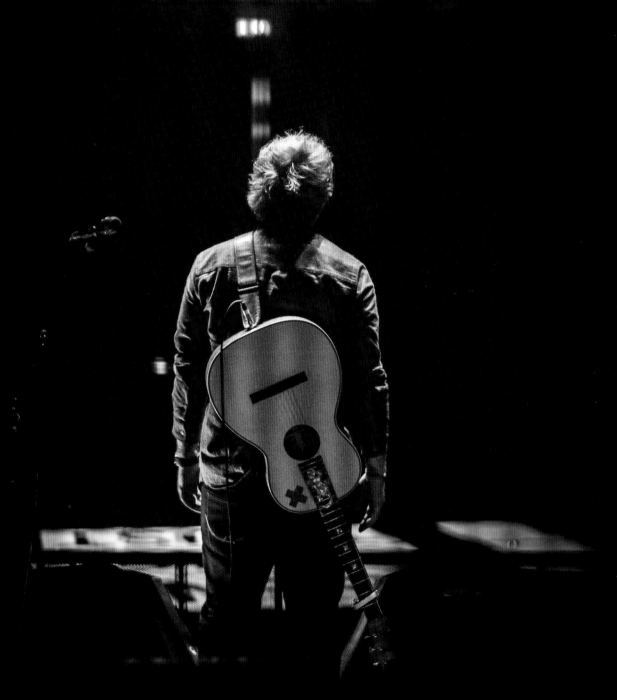

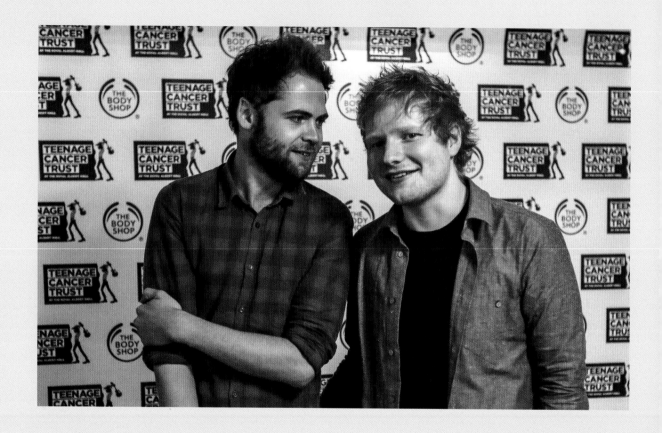

John Sheeran

This is a great shot of two close friends, Passenger (Michael Rosenberg) and Ed. They first met playing a tiny gig for 20 people in the basement of the CB2 Bistro in Cambridge, UK, when no one in the music industry was showing any interest in their work. You can see the delight on their faces as, just a few years later, they are about to go on stage at the Royal Albert Hall, London. Passenger and Ed started out as buskers and have both since toured the world and won Ivor Novello Awards for their songwriting.

hard in small clubs. It was really nice to reconnect with them. We had a little chat and reminisced about where we had first met and how things had evolved since then. We actually talked about jewellery, too, as I just love Imogen's designs. We hugged and promised to stay in touch.

Ed's debut performance at the Albert Hall that night was electric. Shooting Ed at "my" hall was all the more special. Ed just raised the royal roof that night, so to speak. He had the crowd eating out of his hand. I snapped myself silly and raced all over the place, from the organ to the circle level, all the way to the top of the hall and back.

Just as I discreetly crept on the stage and navigated myself behind the stage decor, Ed launched into one of his biggest hits, "The A Team", his final song of the night. He encouraged his crowd to use their phone lights to create a magical atmosphere in the hall.

I couldn't believe my luck. I was in the right place at the right time. I placed myself between two light towers and waited for my moment. Ed got up on a stage monitor and commanded the crowd like a maestro directing a symphony. When the chorus kicked in, the crowd sang along, almost like it was a hymn, while thousands of tiny stars waved to the rhythm of the music. That was the moment I had been waiting for. I clicked a couple of frames and hoped for the best, because as soon as he jumped off the monitor the moment was gone. It can be tricky to capture the difference between the subject bathing in strong stage light up front, against a darkened hall in the background with only twinkling phone lights as a light source. It's one of those shots where you don't really get a second chance, and your camera settings have to be perfectly set in advance of what you hope will happen. But somehow, I knew I got it. After two exhilarating fun-filled hours I walked into the soft spring evening with way too many pictures on my memory cards, as per usual. Shooting Ed's debut at the Albert Hall was a moment where the stars aligned for me, the perfect act in the perfect house with the perfect crowd. It just doesn't get any better than that. A couple of days later I got a lovely email from Ed's parents, which said: "Thank you for capturing Edward just like we know him." And that was just the cherry on top.

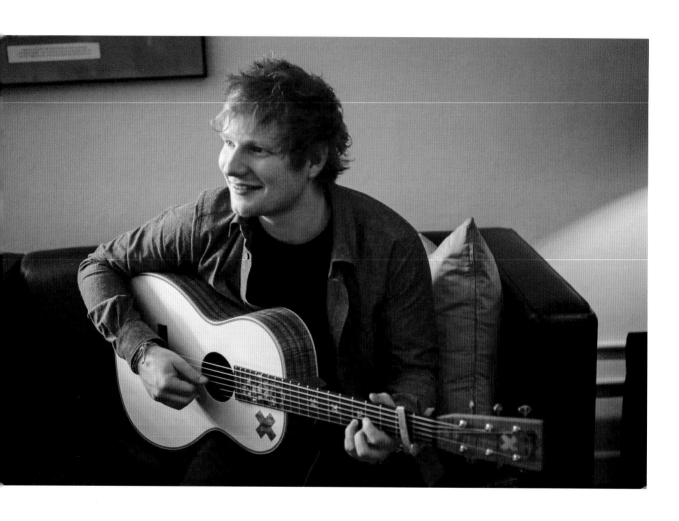

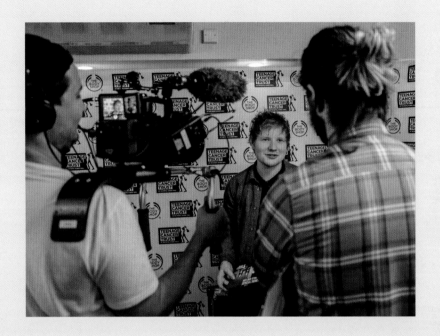

John Sheeran

Ed has given hundreds of interviews throughout his career. Here he is at the Royal Albert Hall,
before his performance for the Teenage Cancer Trust in 2014. He has always been at ease in
front of the camera, being open, honest and positive, and caring little about the way he looks.

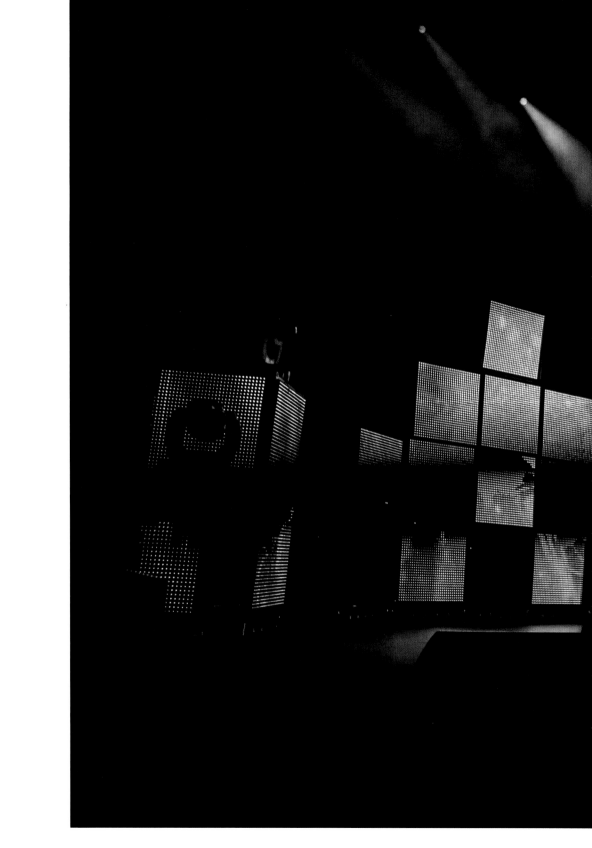

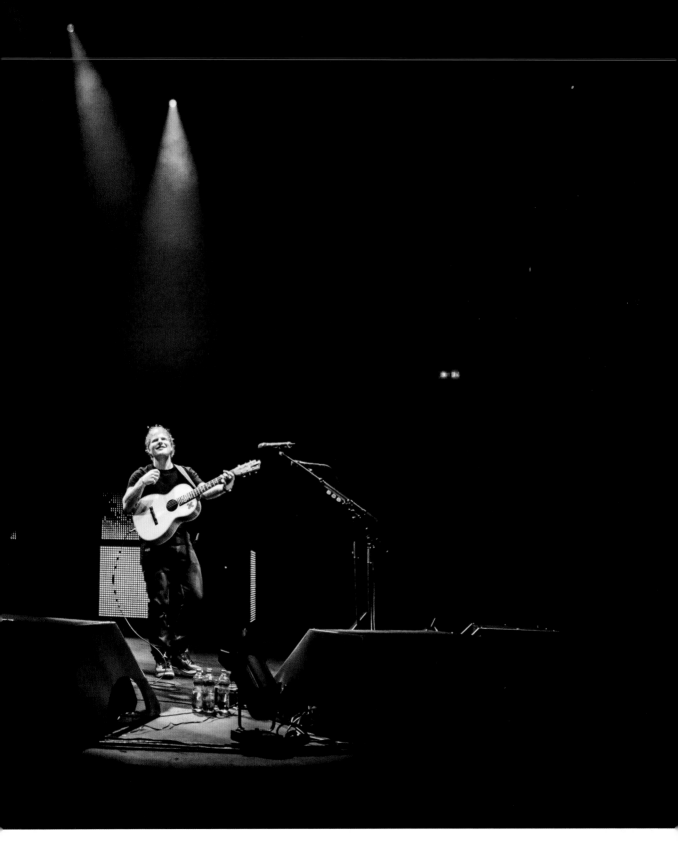

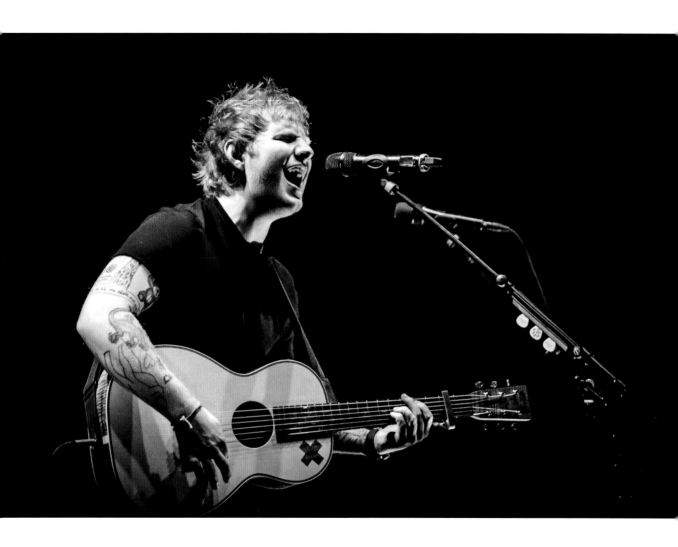

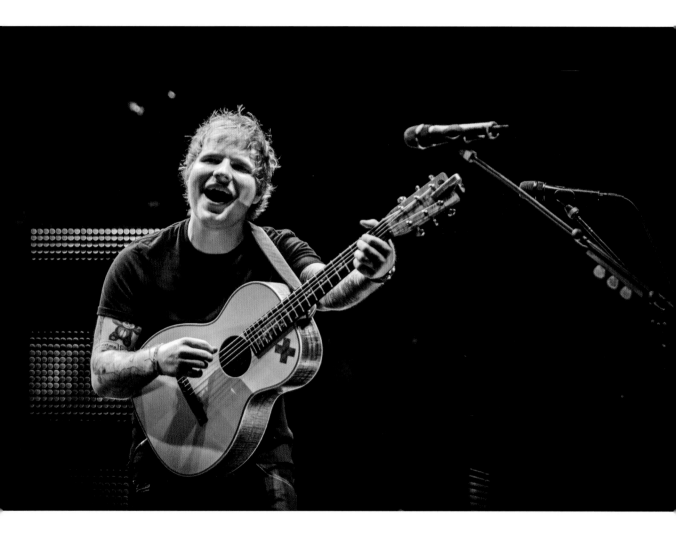

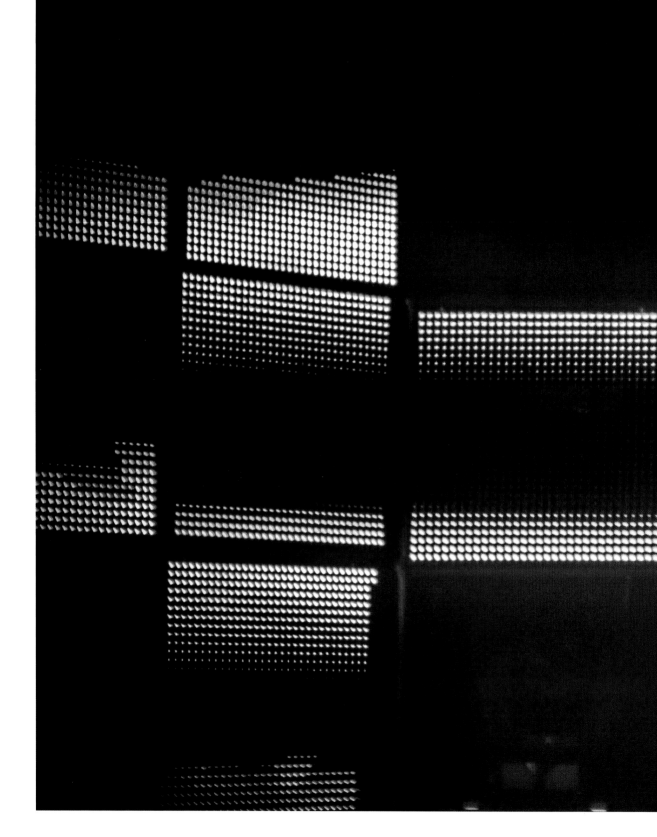

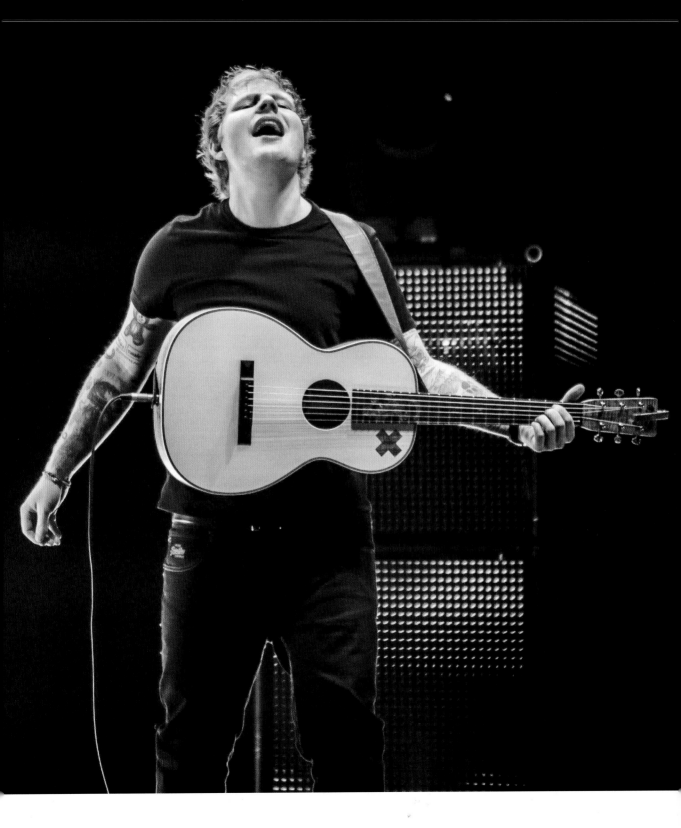

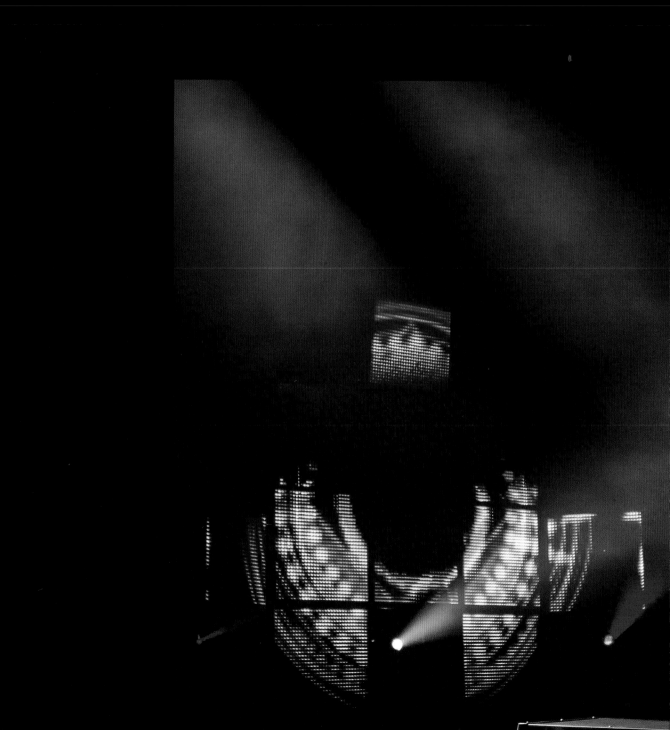

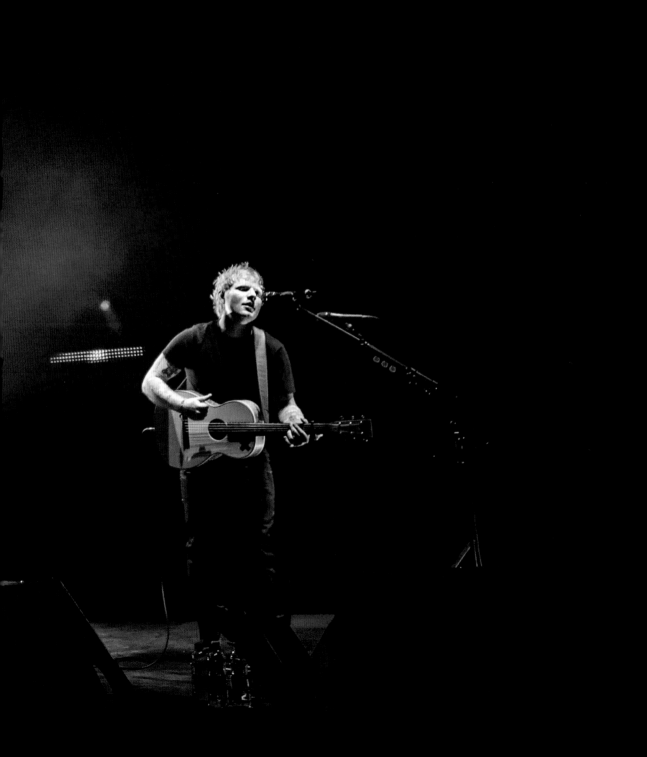

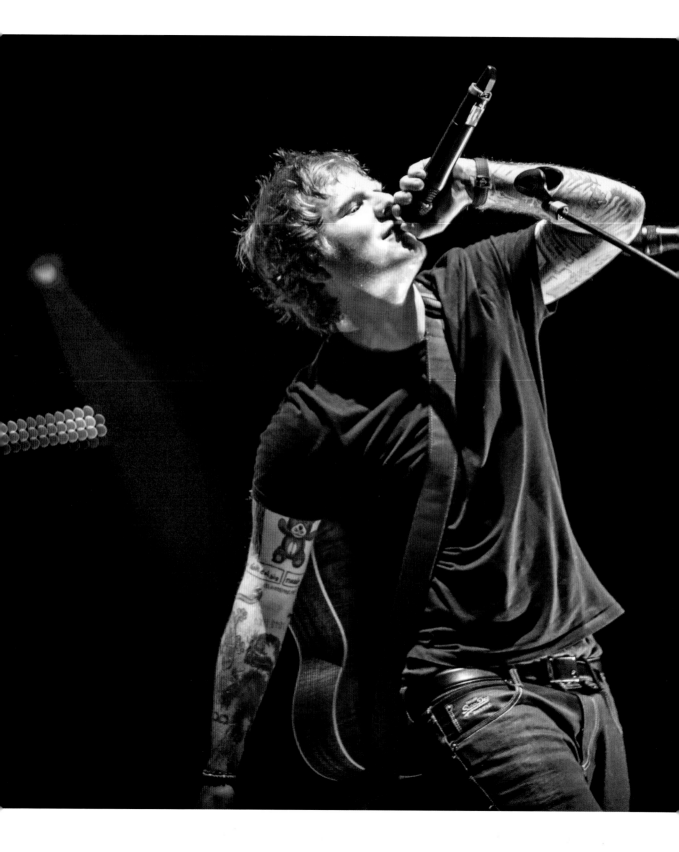

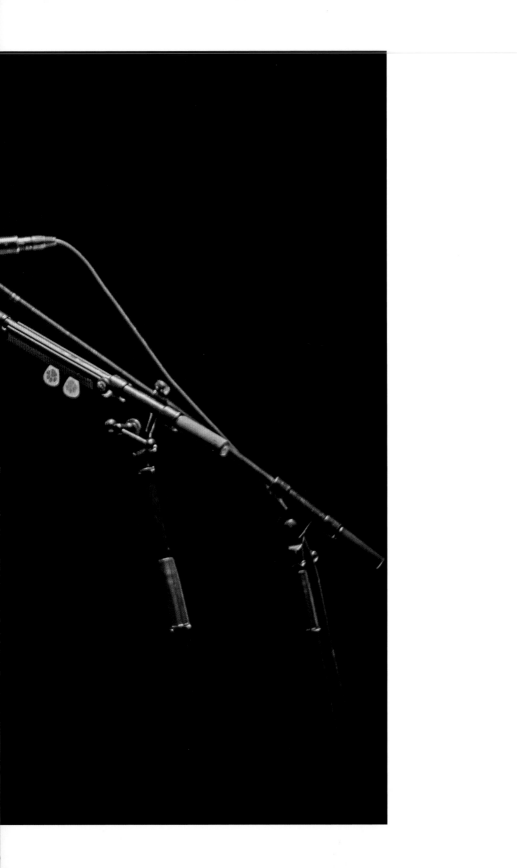

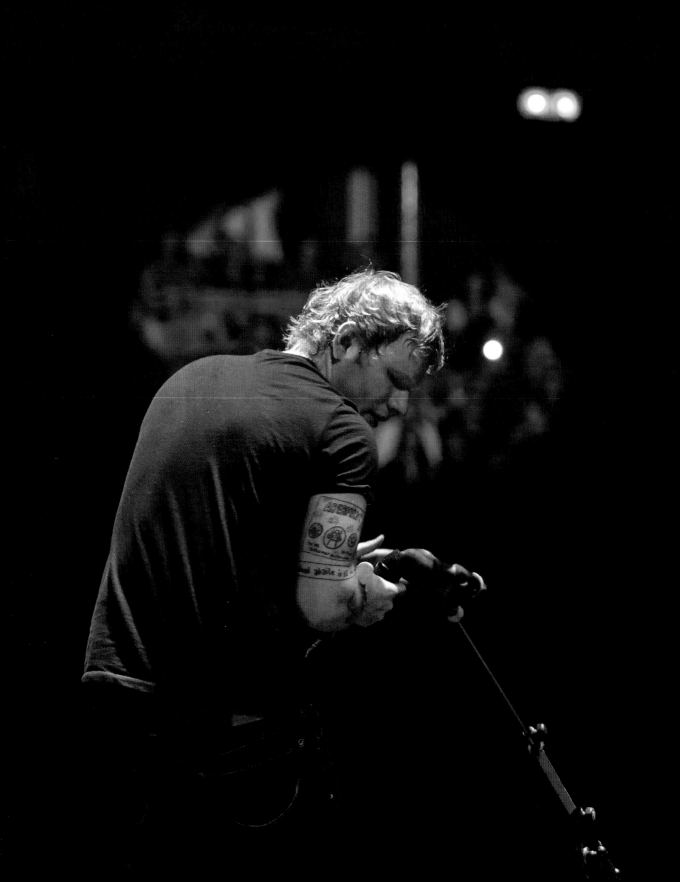

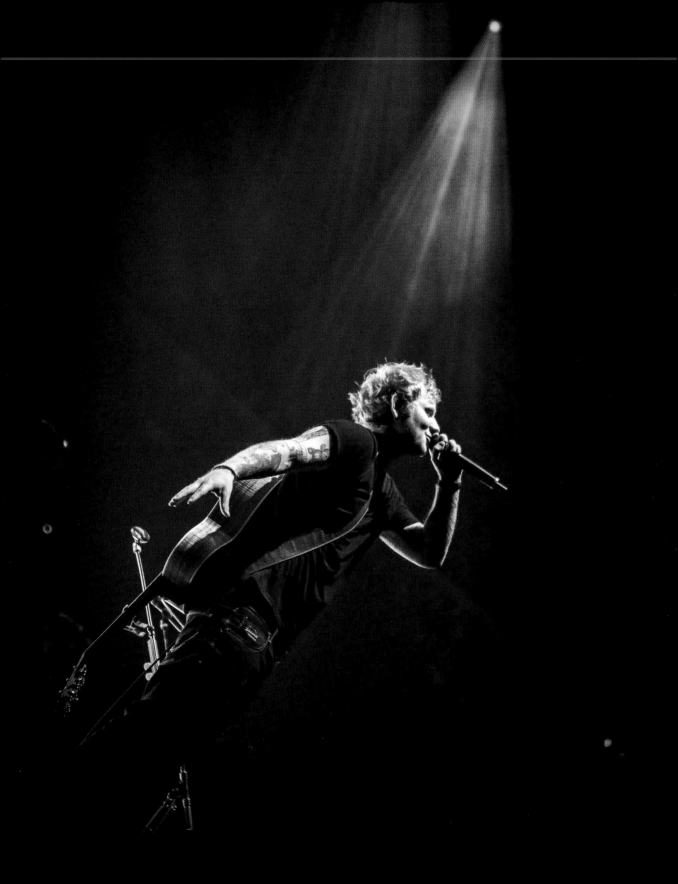

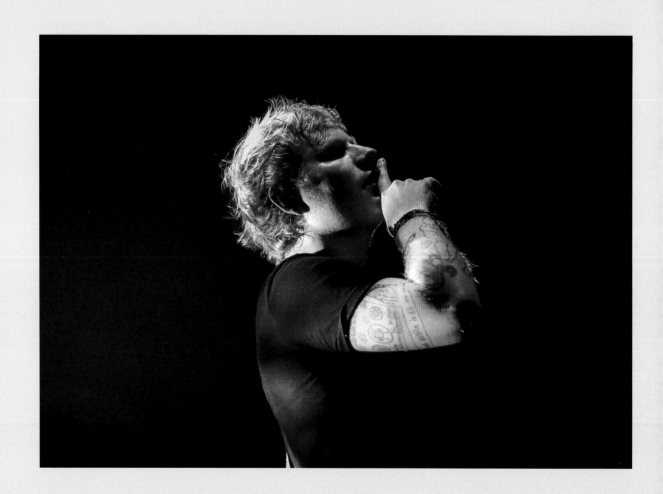

John Sheeran

Ed is putting his forefinger to his lips, hushing the audience at the Royal Albert Hall in preparation for singing a cappella (without any amplification, or instrumental or vocal support). I have even experienced him doing this at Madison Square Garden, in New York City, which has something like three or four times the capacity of the Albert Hall. It takes a lot of courage to attempt such a feat, but Ed thrives on challenges. In the following photo, Ed gives it his all. It shows the physical strain: stripped of its context, it could be read as a primal scream of pain.

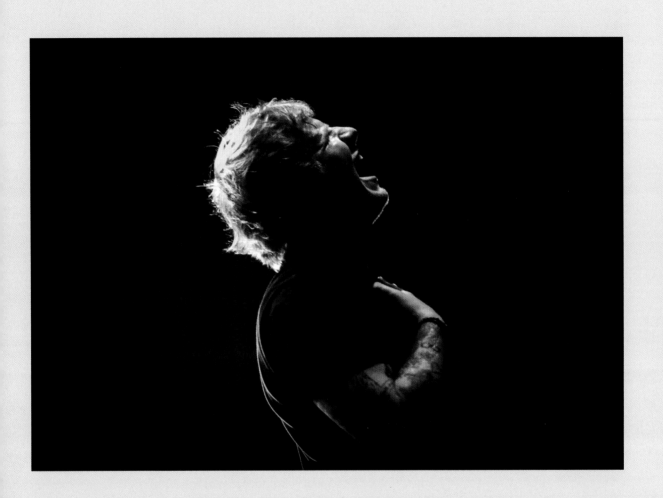

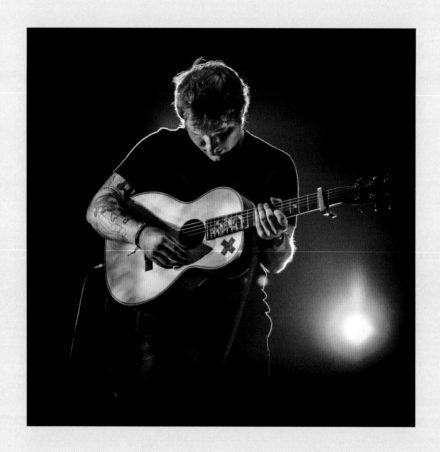

John Sheeran

This is another of my favourite photos of Ed. Like so many of Christie's photos, it looks as though it must have been posed in a photographic studio, and yet it is a moment onstage captured in the heat of a performance that she makes arrestingly permanent. Christie knows instinctively where to place herself and what angles and compositions will work best. Here the spotlight that is trained on Ed throughout the performance is like a ghostly presence. It's as if its light draws the outline of Ed's figure and moulds his form.

142

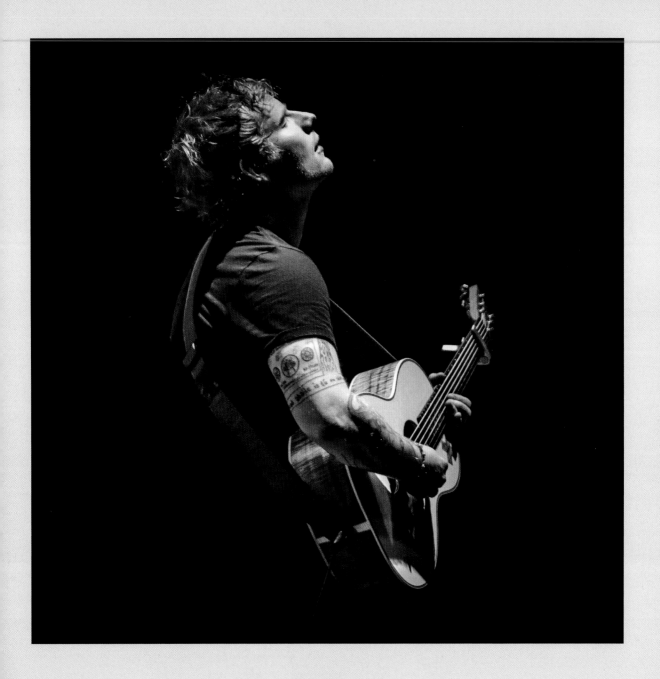

John Sheeran
Here Ed is caught in a moment of musical ecstasy. This is a
superb photo – a classic.

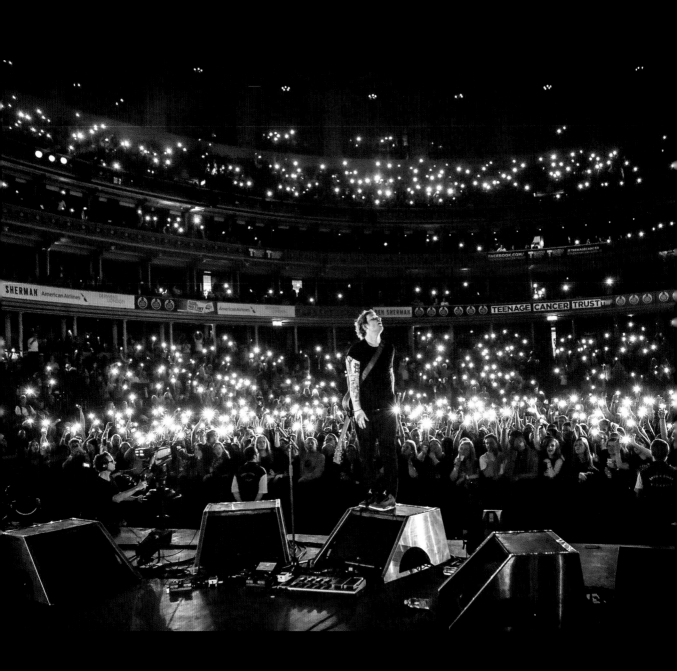

Christie Goodwin

This Royal Albert Hall shot is one of those moments which can often be a gamble to get it right. You have to find the right settings so the subject up front is not over-lit and the crowd in the background isn't too dark. You don't have control over the lights held up by the crowd either. I've shot shows when the lights were not equally balanced, or a large part of the crowd didn't put on their lights, and that just ruins the effect. In this shot, the lights are evenly balanced and I had my settings just right, which makes this shot a success.

Overleaf

John Sheeran

I first took Ed to the Royal Albert Hall in 2004 when he was 13 to see Eric Clapton. We managed to get seats close to the stage and Ed was completely mesmerized by the performance, staring intently at Clapton's acoustic and electric guitar playing to learn as much as he could. It was a hugely influential experience for him. Ed supports various children's and teenage cancer and hospice charities, so when the Teenage Cancer Trust asked him to perform for them at the Albert Hall in 2014, he jumped at the opportunity. My wife Imogen and I went to the gig, visiting him in his dressing room a couple of hours before he went onstage. But we didn't stay long as there was a queue outside his door of teenagers with cancer, some in wheelchairs, accompanied by close family members and friends. Ed had agreed to see all the families one by one for a chat and photos. Then with only a brief break to get ready, he appeared onstage to an incredible roar from the audience. It was deeply moving. These photos perfectly capture the contrast that night between his explosive, raw energy and his hushed, more contemplative side. The whole event was like some sort of triumph or celebration of the human spirit in the face of adversity. It was unforgettable.

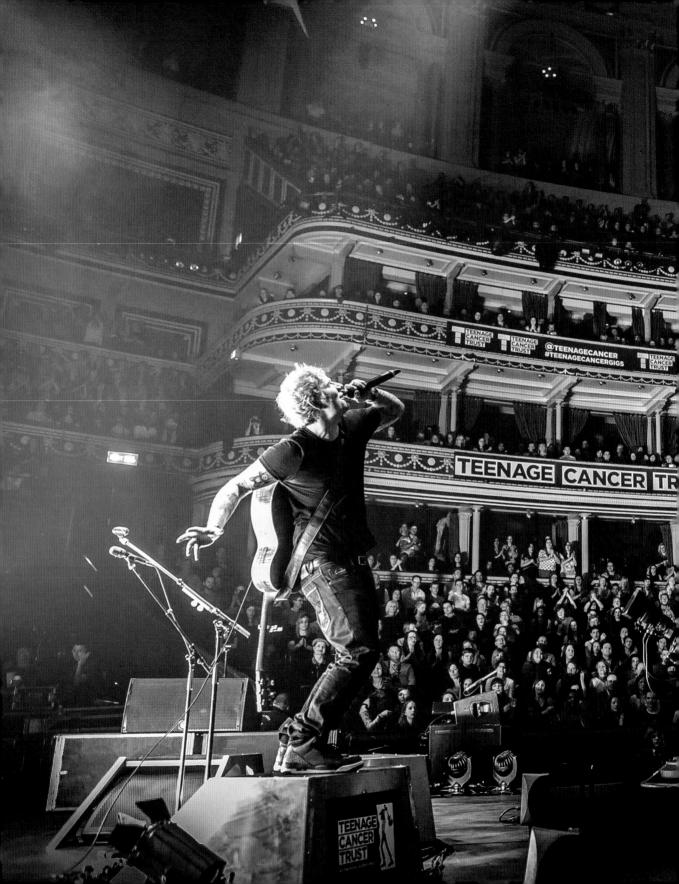

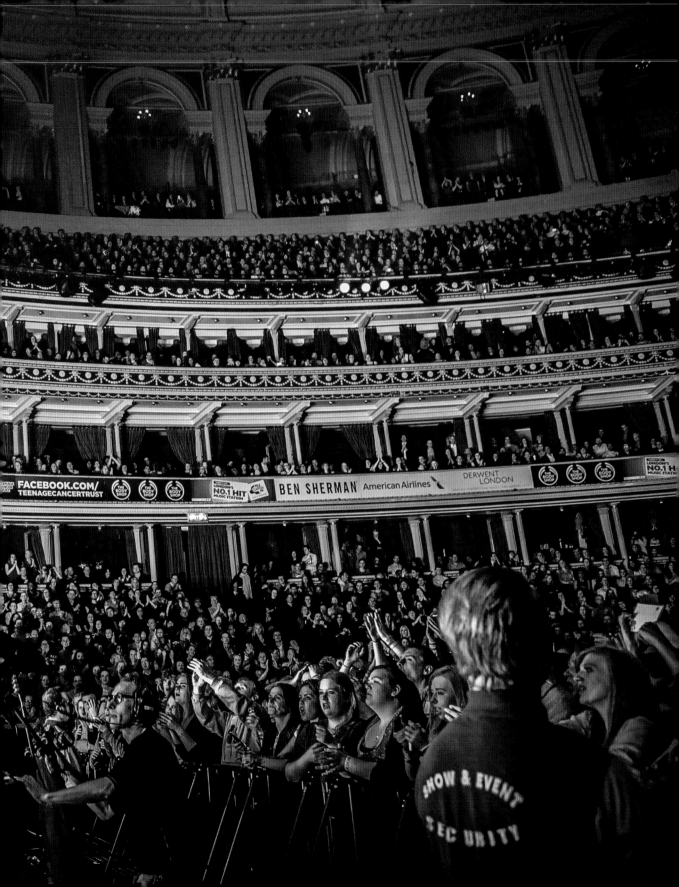

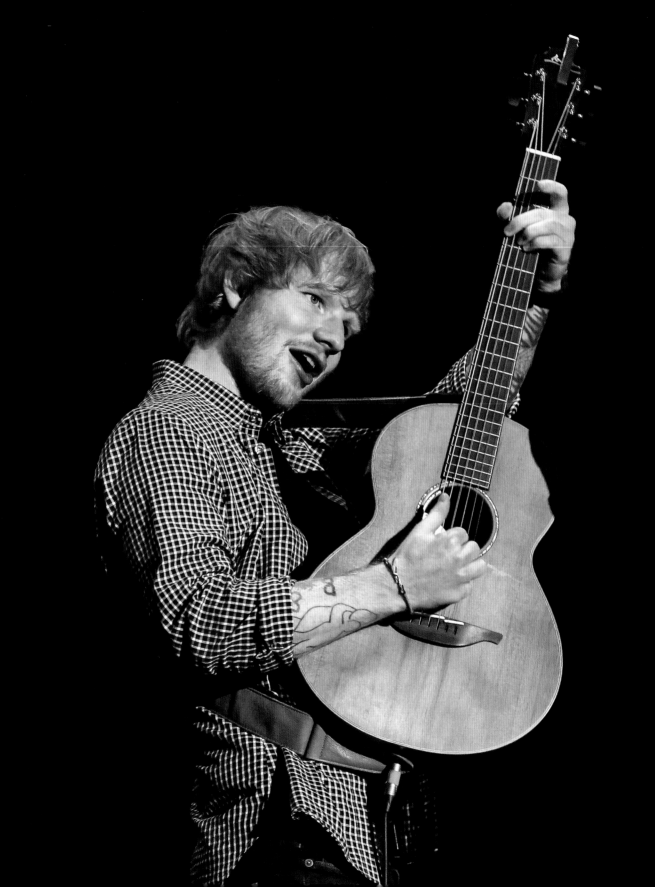

the o2 arena

▬▬▬

UNDER THE MILLENNIUM DOME

I am often asked which equipment I use when shooting live shows and instead of listing it all I usually reply that it doesn't really matter what you shoot with, because there is no one-size-fits-all camera or lens for shooting live music. You start with the notion that you are a conceptual artist who has chosen a camera as their tool. Just like a painter will choose their favourite brushes and a sculptor will choose their preferred materials, you have to explore what works best for you. It will take some experimenting but it's the only way forward. You need to find the camera and the lens that allow you to capture the scene the way you want to capture it. And there's no foolproof method to shooting a concert either. You have to adapt to the genre of music, the size of the venue, and the quality and amount of stage lights.

And that is exactly why I love music photography. No matter how well prepared I am, I never really know what will get thrown at me. It's the mix of challenging lighting conditions, constantly moving musicians and the unexpected kick in the back of your head from the crowd surfer as you try to capture the pure, unfiltered energy of a live performance that makes this job so exciting. That is where my adrenaline kicks in. Some like to bungee-jump and I like to challenge myself in the pit.

I've been shooting live concerts on a professional level for almost 15 years now. I've shot in basements and I've shot in arenas. You'd think I'd cracked the riddle by now of how to be fully prepared when I walk into a pit. Well, I haven't. More often than not I find myself swearing and sweating to conquer the monster. By the time I walk out of the pit I want to have the feeling that I have captured images that will evoke an emotion when others look at them. Music onstage is

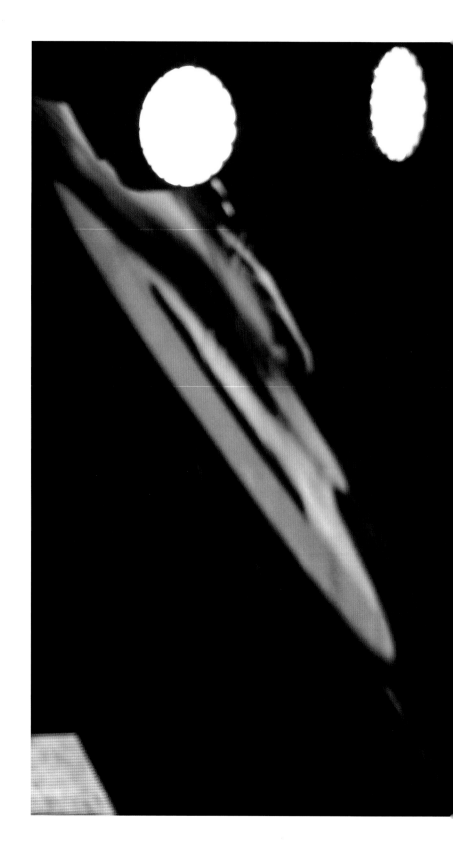

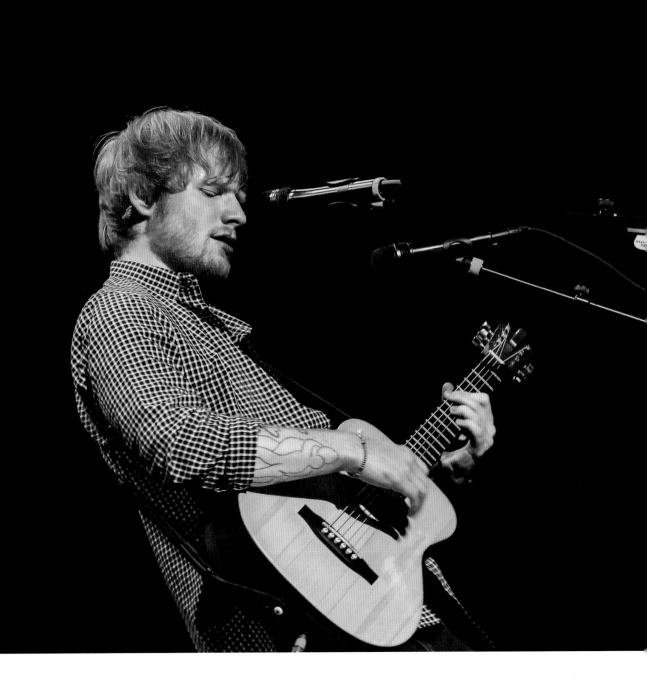

passion and emotion. The only way you can translate the full experience in a single image is by capturing exactly that.

Performing at The O2 Arena in London is as big as it gets indoors on UK territory. Many artists aspire to perform at the arena because of its reputation. With a capacity of 20,000, it's one of the busiest arenas in the world. It opened in 2007 under the Millennium Dome, which is basically a big tent on the banks of the River Thames in Greenwich, in which seven years earlier the government had housed a big *Millennium Experience* exhibition that nobody was interested in.

Ed had already played just about every other venue in London; he now had to conquer The O2 Arena. I was assigned to shoot Ed's O2 debut for press. Outside, the queues were epic, to say the least. As I walked from North Greenwich underground station towards the venue, I was surrounded by a sea of giddy fans, many of them carrying homemade cardboard signs. I remember one sign said: "Ed, I want to have your baby."

I picked up my photo pass and walked inside. There was a buzz in the arena. And then a deafening scream when the lights went out. Ed appeared. "My goal for you is to leave this gig with no voice," Ed told the crowd, and I have no doubt his goal was achieved that evening. They sang every single word and kept screaming in between the songs all the way through. I always wear top-of-the-range ear protection during live shoots, but that evening even industrial-grade ear defenders wouldn't have protected you. They were loud. After the first three songs, the press photographers were escorted out of the pit and for once I wasn't sad to leave the screaming crowd behind me.

On my way out of the dome a string of golden tinsel got stuck to my shoe. It had probably fallen off one of the homemade signs. I picked up the tinsel and hung it around my camera bag while I boarded the Tube train back home. Ed truly is the gift that keeps on giving.

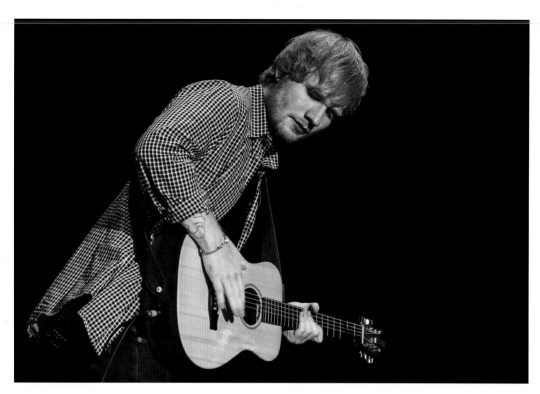

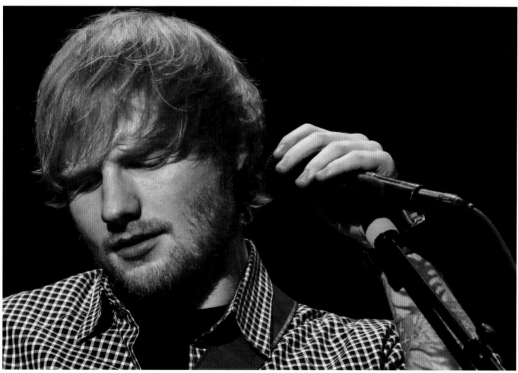

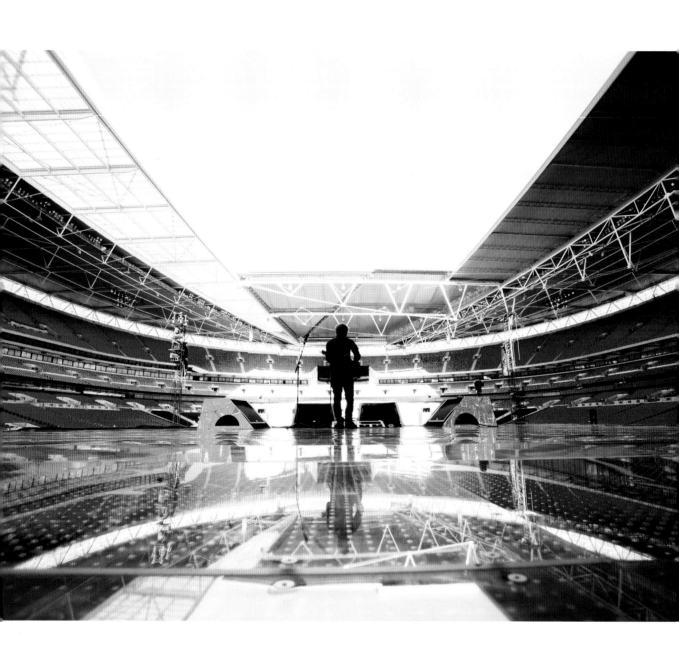

wembley stadium

— LONDON, 9 JULY 2015 —

John Sheeran

This photo shows Ed rehearsing at Wembley Stadium the day before the biggest gig of his life. No one had ever played Wembley entirely solo before. It is difficult to imagine how daunting a prospect this must have seemed to Ed at this particular moment, standing at the front of a vast empty stage, facing tens of thousands of empty seats.

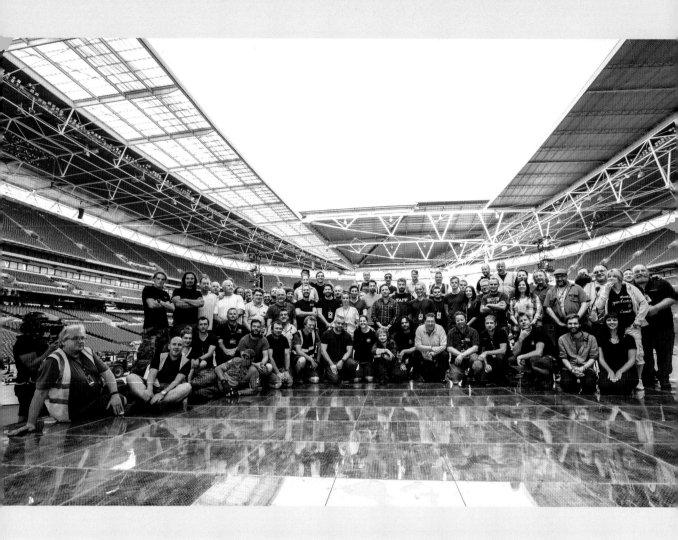

John Sheeran

Here is a photo of Ed's management and crew, many of whom tour the world with him for months on end. They are an extraordinary team, able to work under intense pressure day in, day out, from city to city. They are like one big family, doing fantastic professional teamwork in a positive spirit. Like Ed, for many of them Wembley Stadium in 2015 represented the summit of their careers. I think this group shot wonderfully captures their sense of collective pride and achievement. I can imagine how difficult it must have been to get everyone together for this photo.

WEMBLEY REHEARSALS

I was 14 when I got my very first camera, back in the late 1970s, a Carena 35mm SLR. My daddy bought me this camera because I used to run off with his camera, which he didn't like very much. He was a captain-at-sea, and often I joined him on his round-the-world voyages.

I remember how with my very first roll of film I shot some seagulls that flocked around my dad's ship. As soon I had snapped up the 24 frames on the film, I was impatient to have it developed and see if anything good had come out of it. I still remember the moment I opened the pouch, and the first picture in the pile was a close-up of this majestic wide-winged seagull flying dead centre of my frame. When you looked at it, it made you feel as if it was going to fly right into you. I remember staring at the picture – in awe that I had captured that one-fifteenth of a second in time of a seagull's flight. And that very first picture from that very first film roll is still the reason why I am taking pictures today. To stop time and grasp that one still moment forever – to admire, remember and reminisce.

Fast forward more than 40 years. Many of the jobs I get are last minute. Nobody hires the photographer first. I knew I wanted to be at Wembley with Ed, and I had a gut feeling the call would come. I had several shoots already lined up, but my manager had the same gut feeling and had kept the day of rehearsals and the day of the first show off the books just in case we got the call. And the call came, just two days before Ed's groundbreaking and record-breaking three nights at Wembley Stadium. Ed's manager Stuart Camp basically said I would be responsible for shooting everything, and for delivering photos to his label and the media. Stuart and Ed trusted me to get on with it – it was one thing less for them to worry about.

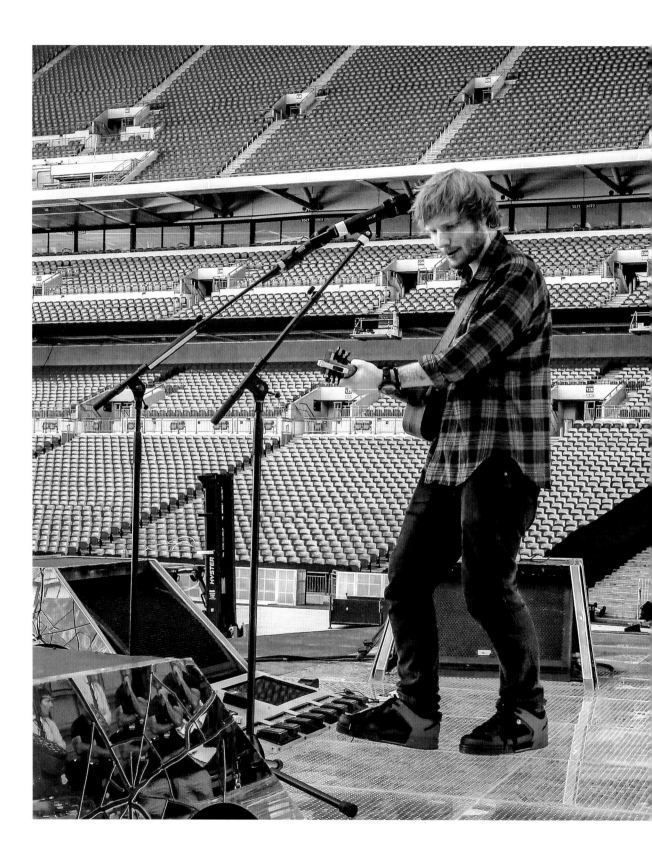

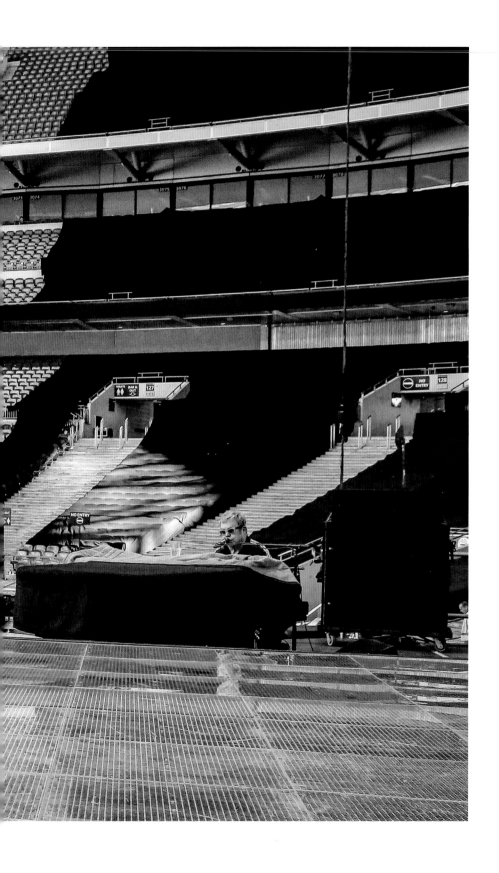

Disappointingly, I wasn't available the other two nights, so I really had to get it right the first time. There would be no second chances. As you can imagine, the thought of being able to record hundreds of moments of what would probably be the defining highlight in Ed's career was both a thrill and an honour.

On the day of the rehearsals we arrived quite early at Wembley Stadium, and as soon as I had walked onto the field, covered in huge metal sheets, it hit me how big this event was going to be. There were crew busy everywhere, finishing the work on the stage, pulling up the lighting rigs, dragging around sound monitors. Forklifts were scurrying over the field, vans kept driving in and out. It was an overwhelming sight. I stood there in the middle of it all with my two cameras, which all of a sudden seemed incredibly tiny, just like me. I was in awe and I couldn't help but feel intimidated by it all. This was it. The next day, on Friday night, Wembley Stadium was going to be packed with 90,000 people to watch one man with a guitar and a loop pedal board single-handedly entertain the crowd for two hours. How amazing was that?

We ran into Mark and Stuart, who explained to us what was happening that day and where I would be shooting from. The beauty was that I pretty much had complete freedom and was allowed to shoot from pretty much anywhere – as long as I got the shots. It was music to my ears.

Ed arrived soon after and walked over the field to look up at the majestic stage – his stage. He turned to us and came over and said hello. We hugged. I asked him if he felt nervous, and he just smiled and said, "Not at all ... yet." I thought he was awfully brave, as I felt nervous and I wasn't the one who had to entertain such a large crowd the following day. I could hide behind my cameras.

I never take pictures of myself with the artist I work for. The artist is the client and I'm the photographer. Do you take selfies with your doctor when you go for a check-up? Exactly! But that day Patrick insisted he take a shot of me and Ed together to document the moment. I reluctantly obliged. Ed then walked around to the back of the stage and walked up the ramp, and I followed him like a little puppy dog. Trevor, Ed's guitar tech, came to hand him his guitar and together they went over a couple of details. Trevor remained by Ed's side while Ed hit his first chords. The sound check with Ed was the ideal time for me to shoot some clean shots on that magnificent stage in that impressive stadium in broad daylight.

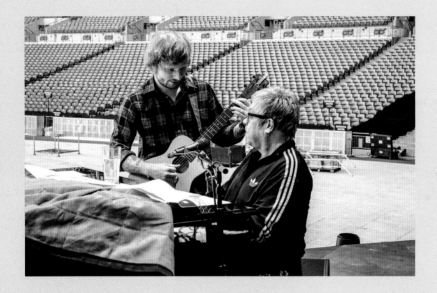

John Sheeran

I am so pleased that we selected Christie's photos of Ed rehearsing and performing with Elton John at Wembley Stadium for this book. Elton has had a profound influence on Ed as a trusted mentor over several years, encouraging and supporting him. Imogen and I cannot thank him enough. Ed has learned so much from him about developing his career, navigating the machinations of the music industry, and coping with the negative aspects of fame. You can tell from these photos that Ed and Elton have a strong professional respect for each other, and a very close personal bond and friendship. They are rehearsing two songs – one by Elton, "Don't Go Breaking My Heart", originally a duet with Kiki Dee, and one by Ed, "Afire Love", written as a moving memorial to his grandfather, my father, who died in 2013. The rehearsal photos reveal their serious intent, as they are both determined to achieve the best for each other. The shot of Ed walking away from Elton back to his microphone shows his absolute focus and concentration on the task in hand. And then, when the rehearsal is over and they can relax, Ed gives Elton an all-embracing thank-you hug.

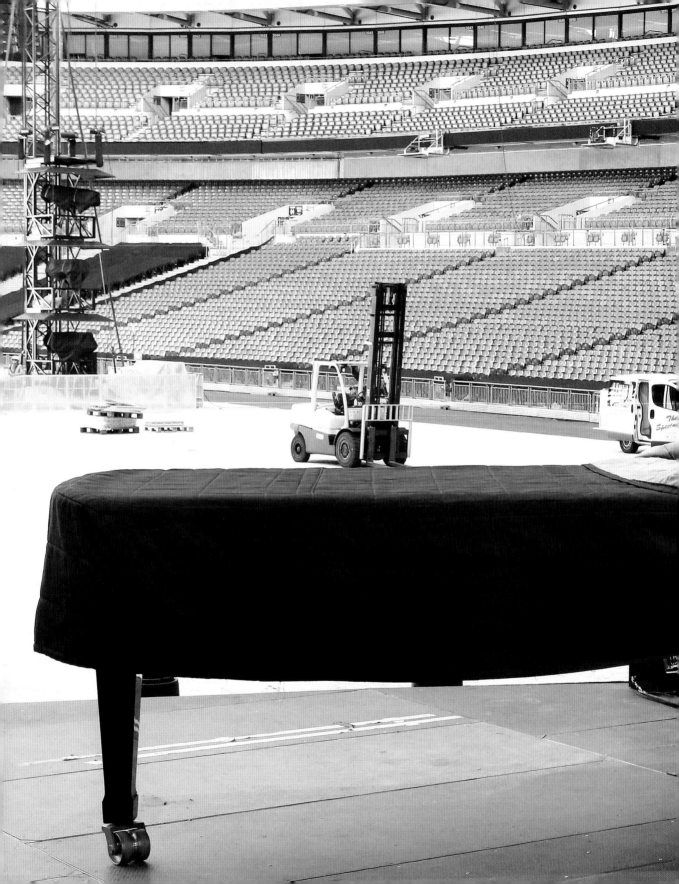

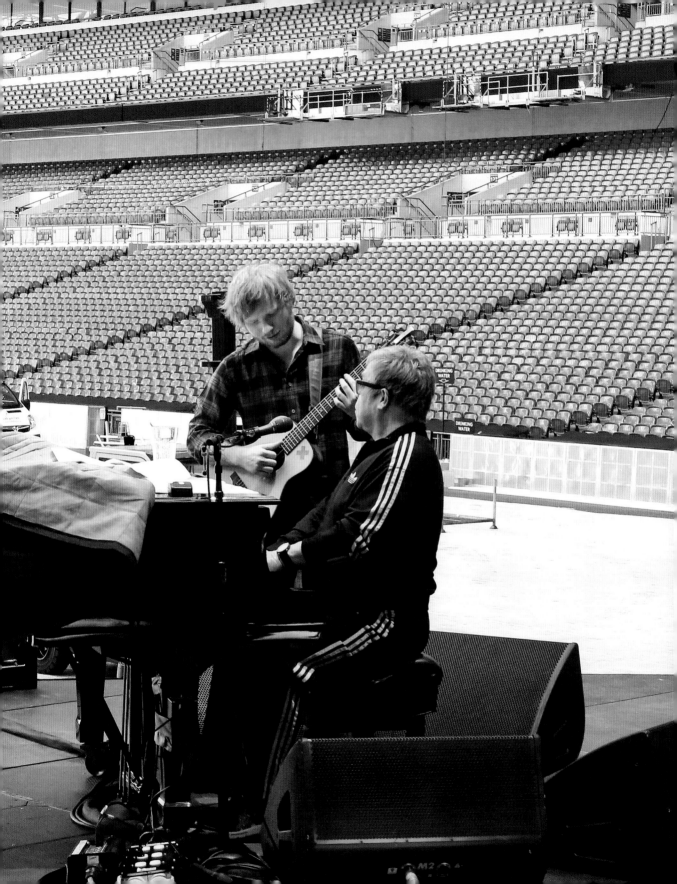

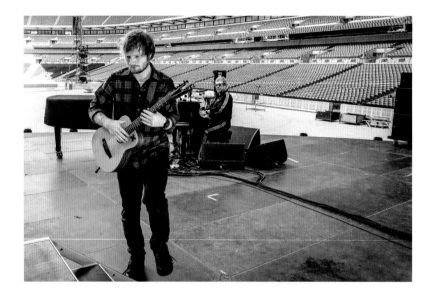

Suddenly, Elton John appeared out of nowhere and went to sit behind his piano. I had wondered why that piano was there. He waved and Ed walked over to hug his friend. They had a little chat, Ed took up his guitar, and together they started figuring out how they were going to perform a unique rendition of "Don't Go Breaking My Heart", Elton's famous duet with Kiki Dee. I kept shooting, but a few minutes later I just couldn't help myself, I just had to tap and sing along.

After the sound check Mark gathered the whole Ed Sheeran team together for a group photo on stage. People kept popping up and Mark kept telling me, "Not yet ... we're still waiting for someone." In the end, it was quite an impressive group. Some of the faces onstage I knew, they had been with Ed for years. I was pleased not just for me, but for them as well, that I could capture all the people together who had made this event happen, on such a majestic stage, with the epic stadium behind them. You don't always realize when you attend a performance how many people behind the scenes have busted their arses off to make it all happen. Each and every one of them has a crucial role in bringing the show to life. It also struck me how everyone was quite calm, but, like they say, calm before the storm.

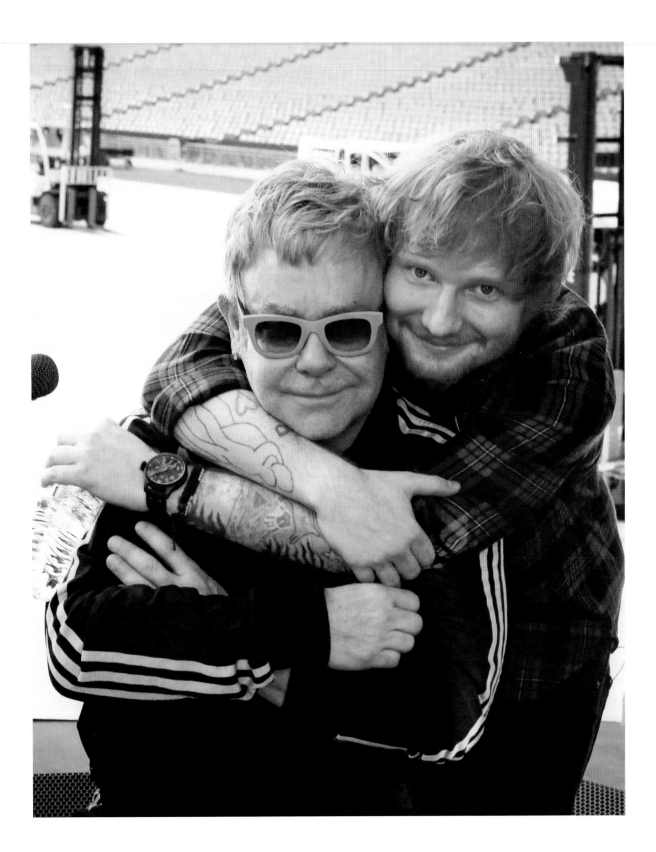

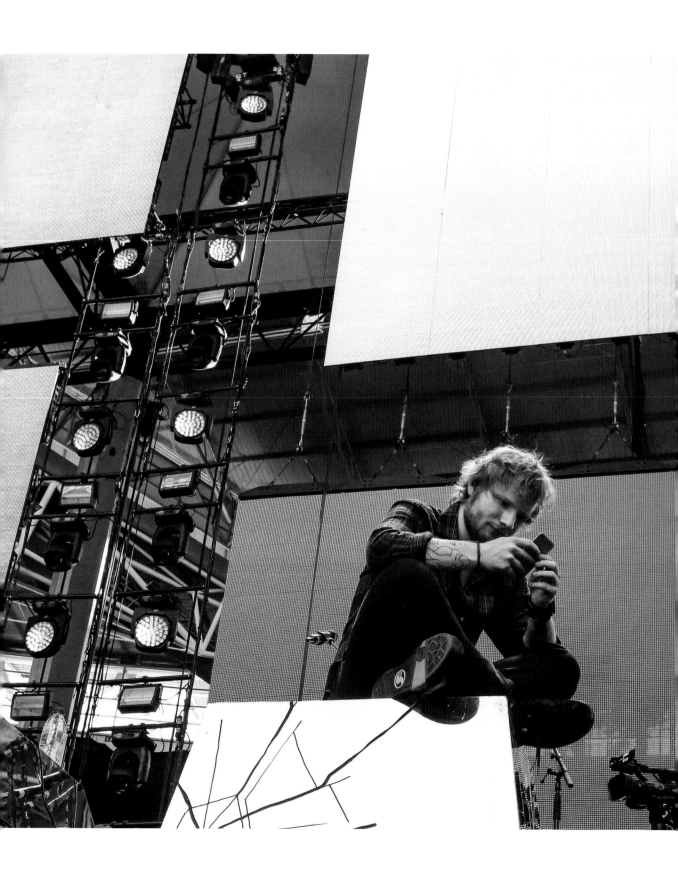

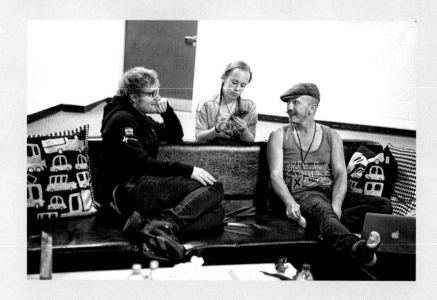

John Sheeran

Ed rates Foy Vance as one of the most gifted contemporary singer-songwriters and performers he has worked with. Foy is also one of the closest friends Ed has made in the music industry. They have worked together a great deal and there is a deep understanding, trust and respect between them. Ed especially admires Foy's integrity as an artist. Here they are together with Ella, Foy's wonderful daughter, relaxing in a dressing room at Wembley Stadium in 2015. Foy is about to go onstage as Ed's support act. Rewind back to July 2007, when I drove Ed to the Wye Fayre festival, held in some fields in Kent (UK) where you could also camp. Foy was the last act to perform, around midnight. I remember Ed, aged 16, sitting cross-legged on the grass, just a few feet away from Foy, completely spellbound by his performance. It was definitely a light-bulb moment for him. From then on, he tried to get to as many Foy Vance gigs as he could. In November 2015 Foy signed to Ed's record label, Gingerbread Man Records.

ED RULES WEMBLEY

The following day the atmosphere was quite different. We walked up to the stadium in the early afternoon and there were already thousands of fans around. At the sides of Olympic Way, the avenue that connects Wembley Park underground station with Wembley Stadium, street vendors were selling all kinds of stuff, a lot of it with glitter and flickering lights. There were hot dog stands and ice cream vans. It felt like walking through a carnival. I noticed a lot of younger children accompanied by their parents. Ed attracts a wide range of fans.

Getting inside the building had become more complex as well. The stage entrance gate had been fenced and security went over my roller bag and handbag with a fine-tooth comb before I was allowed to enter. Inside the arena there were no workmen dragging stuff around and the forklifts were all parked nicely backstage. Instead, people were running around nervously, most of them with very serious faces. More security staff were at every entrance, every corner, every gate. This was no longer the calm; this was starting to feel like the storm.

We walked into the artist corridor and met with Mark, who handed me a series of passes I had to wear so I would have unobstructed access. I needed a pass to access the pit in front of the stage, but I also needed a different pass to access the stage itself. They wanted to keep the stage strictly off limits for anybody who didn't need to be there. Everything was meticulously organized.

I hung around in the dressing room area for a bit but didn't walk into Ed's room. Ed was about to do the biggest gig of his life; he didn't need me in there with him. Ed's friend Foy Vance was the support act that day, and Foy's manager had expressed interest in having me take some shots of the occasion, as I was there

169

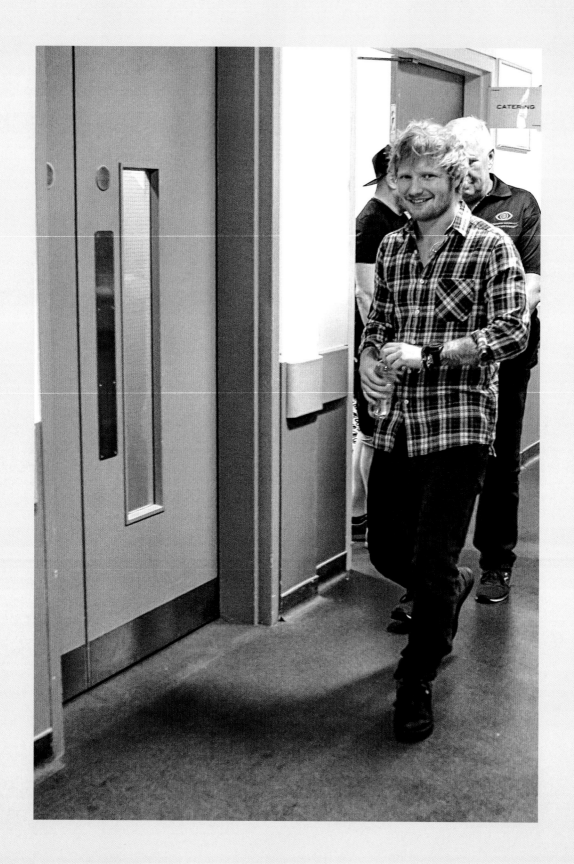

John Sheeran

These photos show Ed making his way from his dressing room to perform on the Wembley Stadium stage for the first time. To begin with it is all smiles, as Ed is accompanied by his security and his tour manager Mark Friend down the corridor. Then, as he strides purposefully through the parking and loading bay, you can sense the tension and nerves kicking in, as Ed can now hear the crowd. He doesn't know whether he will be able to pull off a solo gig in front of 87,000 people, as it's something he has never done before. As he reaches the bottom of the ramp up to the stage, he is greeted by his stage manager, Matthew Caley. They rap knuckles and Matthew looks into Ed's eyes as if to say, "Good luck, mate. Just go for it." Matthew and Ed have been working together for years. In the next shot, Ed and his manager Stuart have their arms around each other in a touching embrace, as Ed is offered some final words of encouragement. The two of them have been on an incredible journey together, and this is the climax of their achievement so far. Finally, in a slightly blurred shot, Ed emerges alone. We can see the crowd in the distance, and now it's all up to him.

anyway. I knocked on Foy's door and he waved me in and we took some candid portraits. Ed walked in a bit later for a chat with Foy. He still seemed quite calm and serene. A little later we ran into John and Imogen who were just making their way to their seats. We hugged and they were obviously excited to see their son achieve such a milestone in his career.

And then the time had come. Showtime! Ed left his dressing room and made his way to the stage with Mark and Stuart by his side. In the corridor, he smiled at everyone and waved to my camera as he passed by. Mark then led him under the north-west stands to the back of the stage. They stood still for a moment at the bottom of the ramp. The stage manager gave Ed some last-minute pointers, and they gave each other a fist bump. Ed and Stuart put their arms around each other's shoulders for a second, and then Ed started his walk up on the ramp with Mark, followed by Stuart. I stood at the top of the ramp. I can't even begin to imagine what must have been going through Ed's head at that time. When he reached the top of the ramp he peeked over at the stage and saw his crowd for the first time. Trevor handed Ed his guitar. Ed was dead serious and looked into the packed stadium. Then, with a very determined step, he walked to the front of the stage. I snapped a few shots from up there as he launched into his gig and then I returned down the ramp to go to the pit in front of the stage.

I thought back to our very first meeting in that club above a pub in Camden where he played in front of no more than 25 people. Now he was here performing three sold-out nights at Wembley Stadium. I felt a little bit disappointed that I wouldn't be able to cover the next two days because of those other commitments. I think I even asked Patrick that evening if there was any way that I could get out of them. I knew it wouldn't be possible, and ordinarily I would never have done something like that, but just for a moment, I admit, I thought about it. I had to enjoy that night for all it was worth.

Once I had entered the pit, I had a bit of a struggle with the stupendous scale of it all. I don't think I've ever felt so small as I did in front of that humongous stage. Me and my two photo cameras surrounded by 20-odd large film cameras placed all over, seriously obstructing my sight when they were rolling from left to right in front of the stage. The stage was so high that at times I could see only the top of Ed's head.

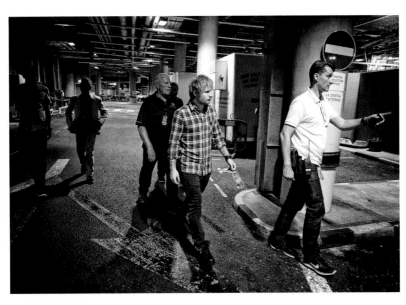

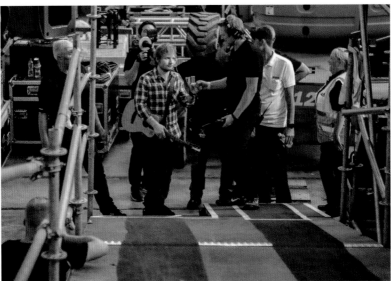

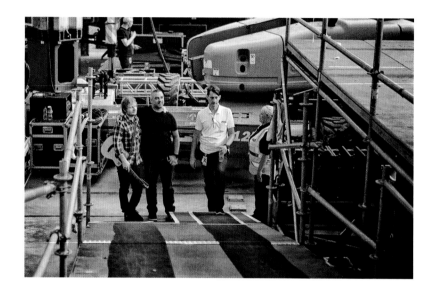

A dozen huge screens were placed at the back of the stage showing Ed with different colours and effects depending on the song and mood. The whole production was larger than life and I felt like a little mouse stuck in an elephant cage. But I couldn't allow myself to panic or get irritated by those roving cameras blocking my view all the time. If Ed could handle it all by himself to entertain the crowd this size without the aid of pyrotechnics, special effects or gimmicks, then I, surely, could do my thing with my two little cameras. I apologize to my cameras calling them small but in the grand scale of things they were minuscule that day.

Halfway through the gig the audience were pleasantly surprised when Ed announced that he would be joined by Elton John. I had already decided to shoot their first song together from the pit and then to go back up to the stage to shoot them with the crowd as their background. At the end of their second song they hugged and Ed continued on his own.

Because my view from the pit was a bit unpredictable, I decided to stay onstage to try to get the perfect iconic Wembley Stadium shot I knew I needed.

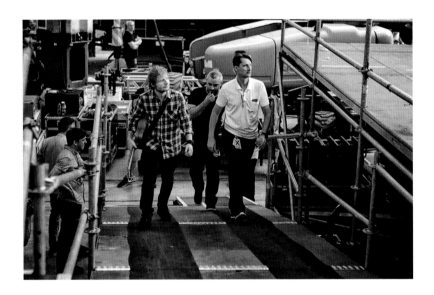

The sun had gone down by now and the spotlights were roving from left to right over the stage, so it took some patience and waiting for the right moment to get the shots I was after.

My highlight that evening was when Ed asked the crowd to hold their phone lights up. I remembered the moment during his Royal Albert Hall gig the year before, so I was ready to capture it. Instantly, the stadium was lit up with a sea of little star lights. Once again, it was tricky to capture as the stage was quite bright and the stadium, despite the phone lights, was quite dark. I kept scrolling my shutter speed from one side to the other and then there was this moment, as if all had gone quiet. The whole stadium was waving their lights – I held my camera very still, pushed the release button and I knew I had it. The shot that would tell the story of that night. The story of that monumental moment for Ed, proof of how far he had come. Before he left the stage, Ed told the crowd, "I will never forget this." And I thought to myself, "You and me both, my friend, you and me both."

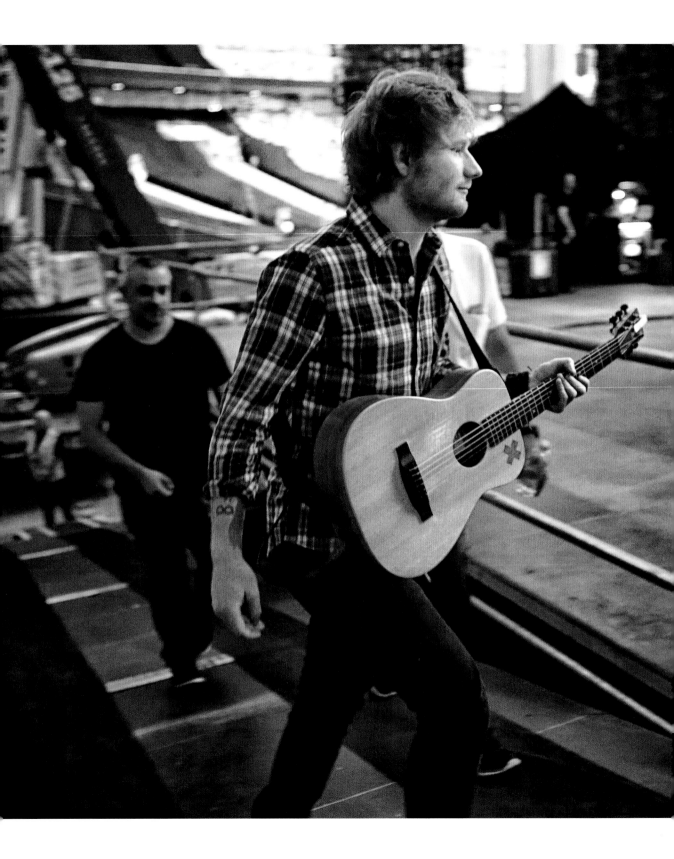

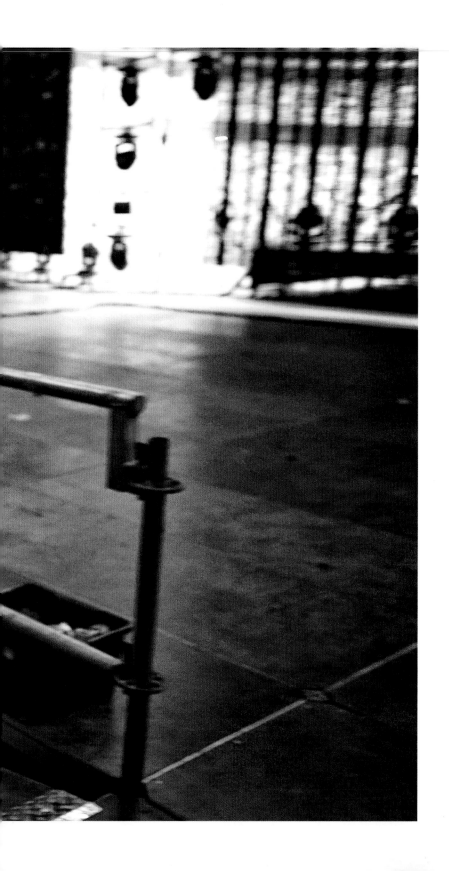

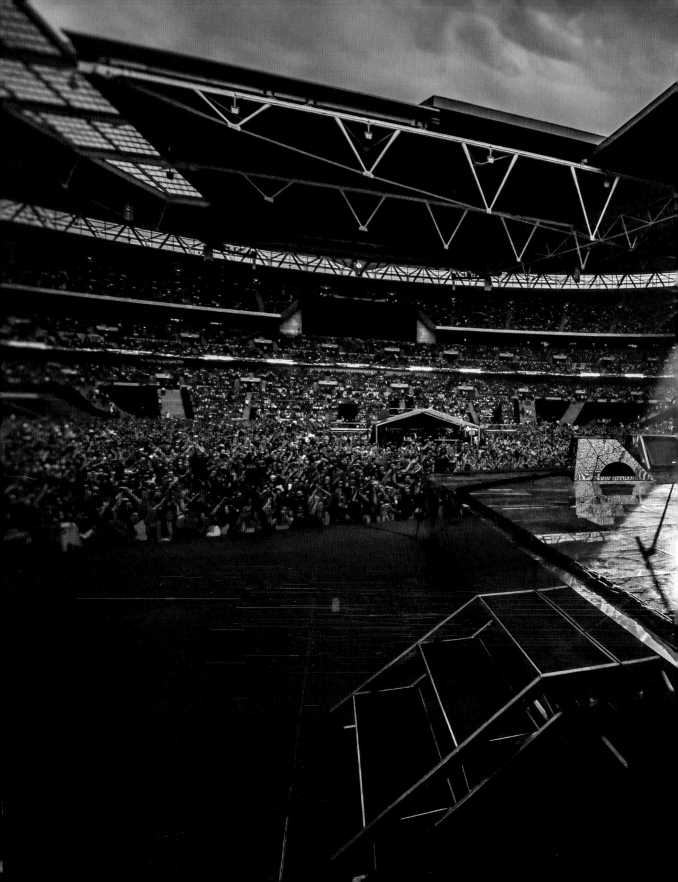

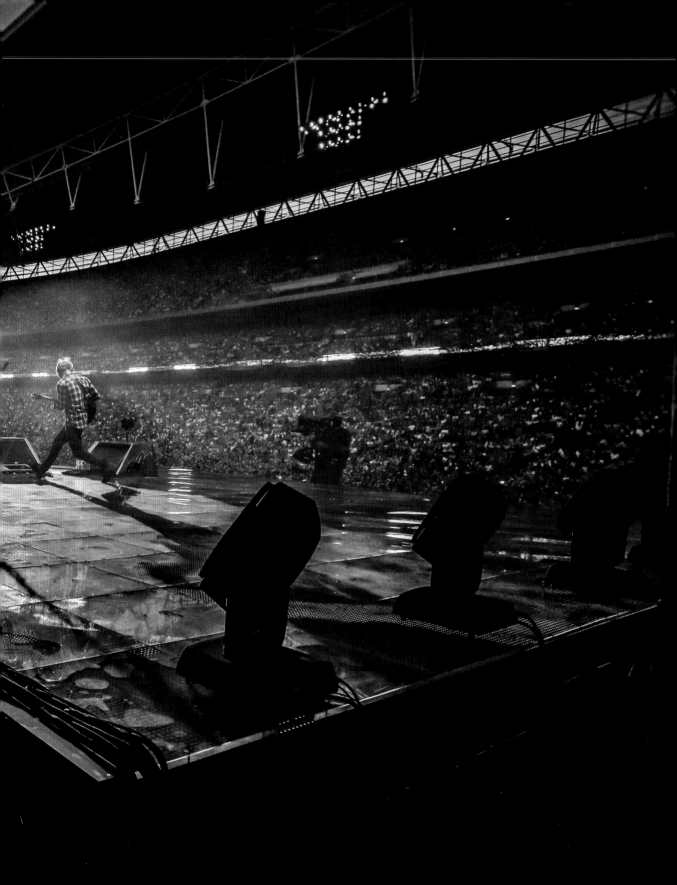

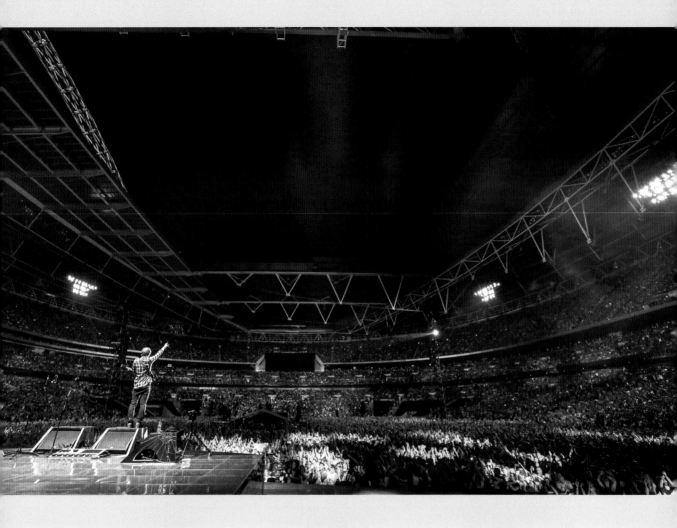

Previous pages

John Sheeran

At last Ed is onstage and he immediately kicks off with a lively opener to get everyone on to their feet singing. The first song and its reception are crucial for setting the mark for the rest of the gig. But there is still daylight. The atmosphere is always greater when it's dark.

John Sheeran

This photo gives a great sense of what Ed experiences from the stage: the frightening immensity of Wembley, the surging movement and energy of an enormous crowd, and a non-stop lighting extravaganza. Viewing this photo, we, of course, can't hear the sound of the music or the thousands of voices singing his words back to him, but nevertheless it powerfully captures the atmosphere and the uniqueness of the occasion.

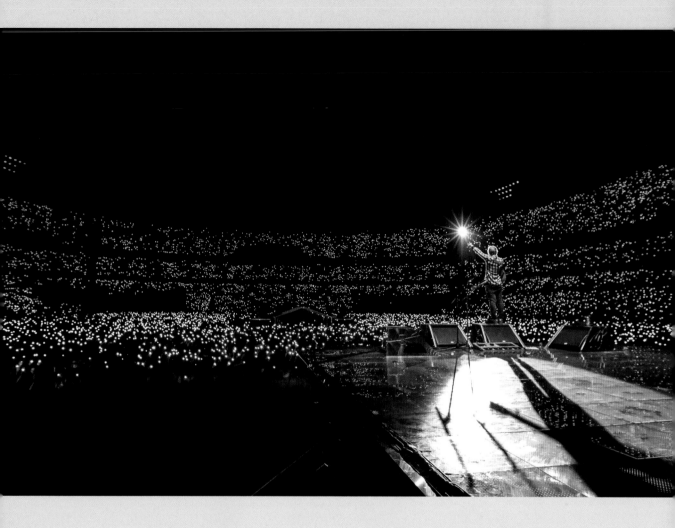

John Sheeran

This is an iconic image that sums up everything Ed stands for. He's performing all alone, commanding a vast crowd, with the lights of thousands of mobile phones shining like stars in a night sky. And the brightest star of all, a distant spotlight, illuminates him and casts his long shadow back over the huge stage.

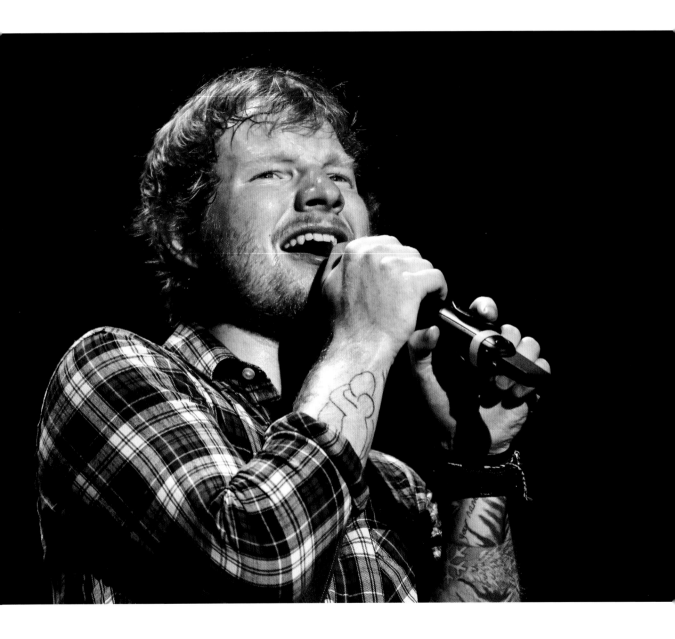

CAPTURING THE ESSENCE OF ED

I am often told: "You really captured the essence of so-and-so in that shot." As flattering as that may sound, I don't buy into the whole "capturing a person in one picture" deal. I can only hope there are many more aspects to me as a person than one single image can portray. We are all multifaceted, complex human beings, and maybe it takes a book full of pictures to capture the essence of a person. When shooting Ed, that has always been my focus. Whether I shoot him live onstage or I am shooting him backstage, performing or posing, they each are a facet of Ed. That is Ed the performer. I also want to capture those moments that make him unique, that make him the Ed I know. You will often find me sitting back and just observing people. When I shoot a live concert from the pit, I never stop shooting because it is often in the moments in between songs, when their performance button is switched off, that for just a second or two I can capture another facet of that person onstage. Those are often the most significant moments to capture if you want to get the full picture. It's all about observing attentively.

Another question I often get asked is: "What makes a great photograph?" I don't think you can answer that. Whatever a great photograph is to you might not be the same to the person next to you. It's very subjective. It depends on your emotions and what you feel when you look at a photograph. A photo can be great because of its structure and composition, because it's set in an enchanting decor, or just because of who is in it and how you feel about that person. Sometimes a photo that I think is great is more about what happened when I was taking the picture: if what I felt comes back when I look at the photo later.

That said, I can give an answer to the question :"How do you learn to take great photographs?" It is all about observing people and what is going on around you. There is a difference between seeing and observing. Most people, when they look through their viewfinder, just see what is right in front of them. I often tell students who want to take up music photography that it doesn't matter whether you have the best equipment that money can buy. If you don't learn to really observe, then that great picture you want to take will escape you.

I'd like to use the example of Ed's first Wembley Stadium show in 2015. For me at that time it was important to shoot Ed in context with the epic magnitude of the stadium he was in. It was the epitome of his career up to that point and that is what I wanted the picture to show. Wembley Stadium is impressive in its size, and the sea of excited fans was just mind blowing. So, I had to just capture exactly that, framing Ed with the imposing stadium as the background. But as I climbed the ramp at the back of the stage and peeked in between the screens and lights, and took in the view, what actually struck me more than the immense scale of the stadium was the size of the stage. It was enormous, a huge surface of some kind of hard transparent plastic, with lights underneath shining up – quite ingenious, with an exciting, futuristic feel to it. It felt a bit like I was standing on the threshold of a sci-fi spaceship. Ed was standing right at the end of the stage near the crowd with his pedal board in front of him. From where I was standing the stage felt just infinite, like there was no end to it. So that was when I decided that what I had to capture was the sheer magnitude of the event. That is why I didn't zoom in more tightly on Ed. I just kept shooting wide-angle shots and let the stage with the stadium as backdrop do all the work. I made sure that, as much as possible, I had almost the whole stage in my frame, and left it bleeding off the frame left and right. That shot where almost half the picture is taken up by the immense stage encapsulates the importance of what happened that day. That was Ed conquering Wembley Stadium.

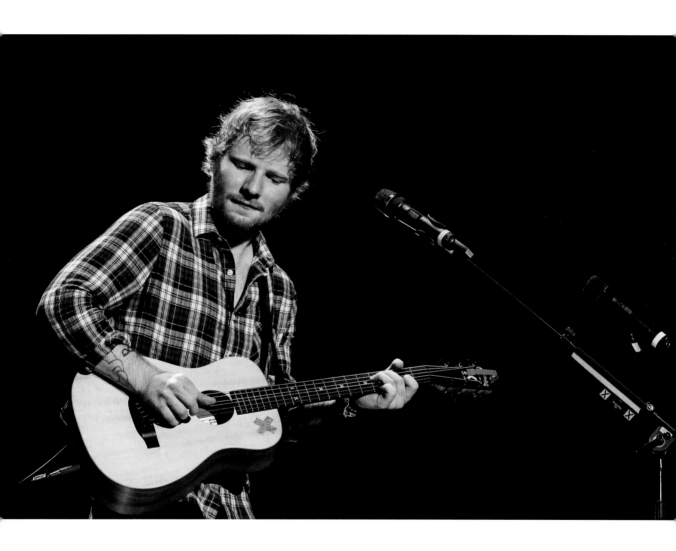

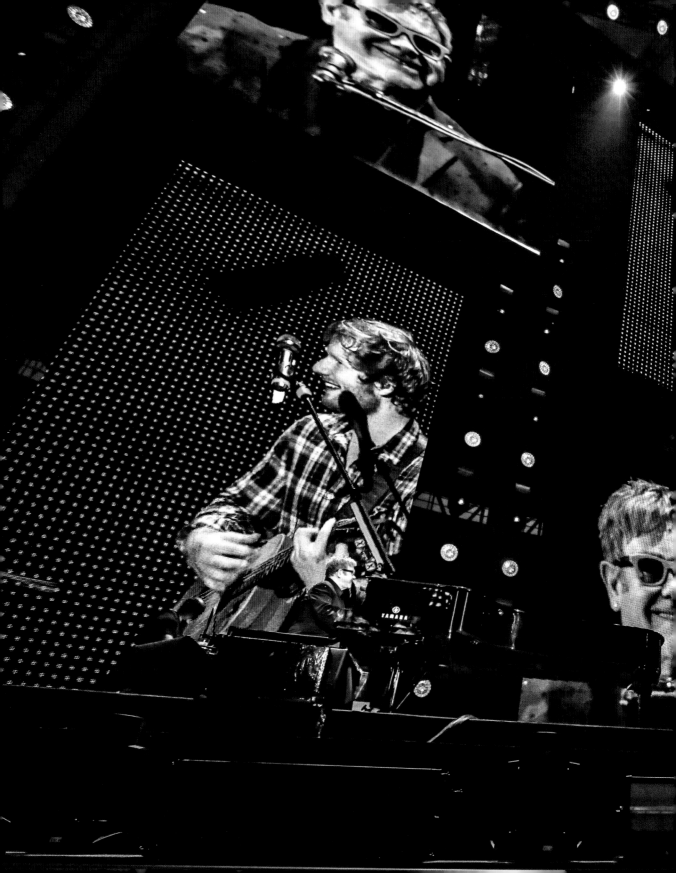

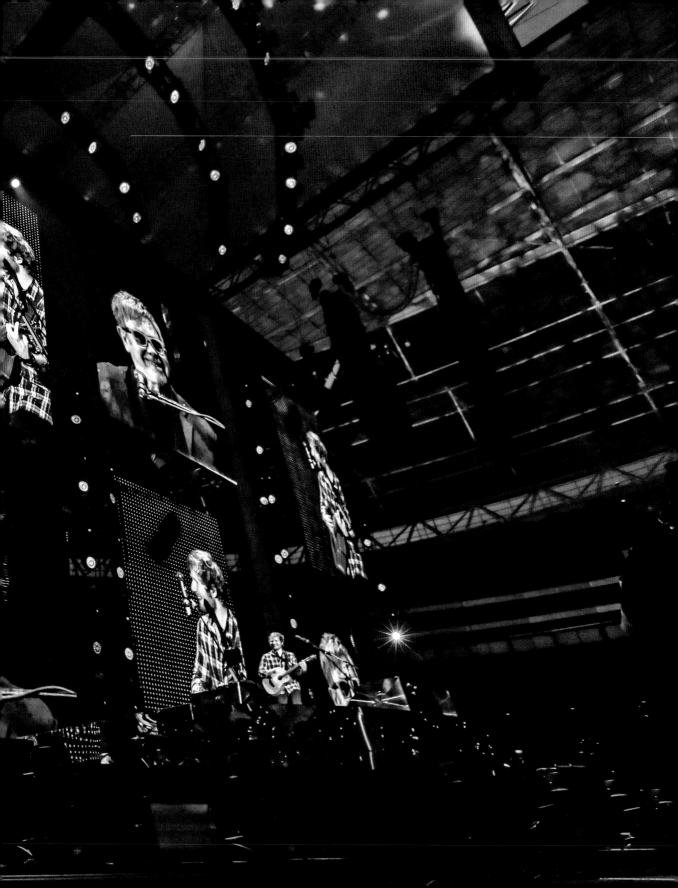

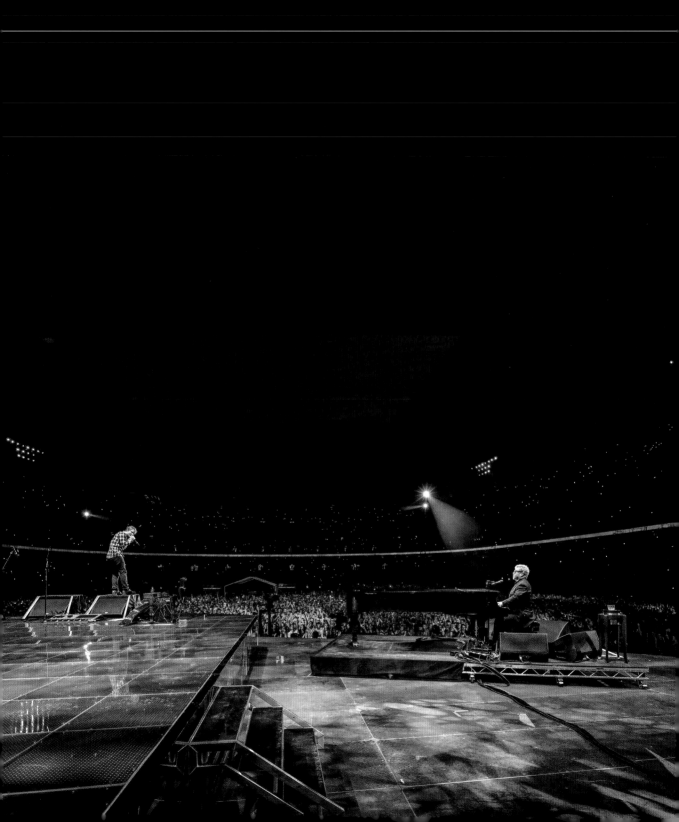

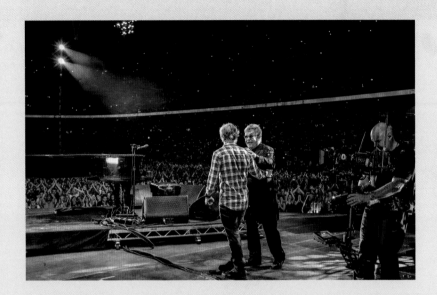

John Sheeran

It really doesn't get any better than this: seeing your son perform at Wembley with Elton John. I remember vividly the incredible reception Elton got from the crowd when he joined Ed onstage. And when they started to sing "Don't Go Breaking My Heart", I sensed a heartfelt exhilaration sweeping through the vast stadium. The shot of the two of them against the huge backdrop of live screens is magnificent. Both have big grins on their faces and they are obviously having a ball performing together. Then you see them embracing afterward, with the crowd ecstatic in the background, and the cameraman recording it all for posterity. It means so much to me that the heroes of my teens and twenties are now Ed's heroes too. He gets on so well with many of the greats, like Paul McCartney, Paul Simon and Van Morrison, and has performed with Eric Clapton, the Rolling Stones and Stevie Wonder. It is just remarkable.

Left

Christie Goodwin

I've chosen this Wembley picture because I like how we can be a witness to Ed and Elton sharing the stage from up close. Elton John joined Ed for two songs, and the first song I had shot from the pit. After the first song, I ran up to the back of the stage and shot the rest from behind the screens. I waited patiently for this moment when Elton looked up toward Ed and Ed was turned toward Elton. Sometimes, patience is all it takes to get the best shots.

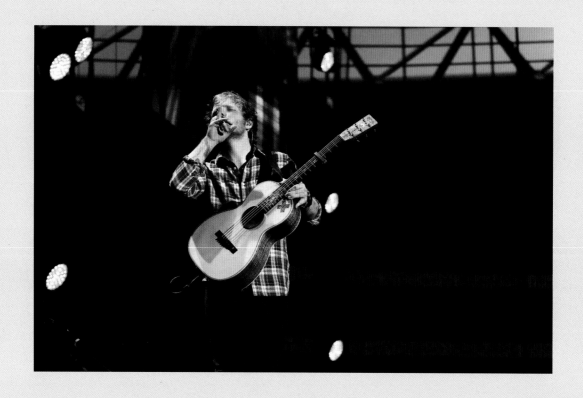

John Sheeran

Earlier in this book, we saw Ed trying to hush the audience at the Royal Albert Hall. Now he is attempting it at Wembley Stadium! This is a photo that illustrates Ed's limitless, positive ambition. Everything seems possible to him.

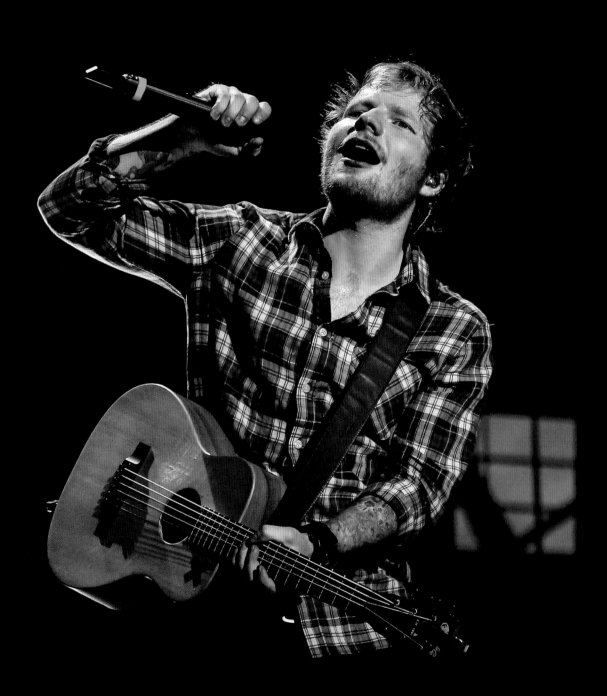

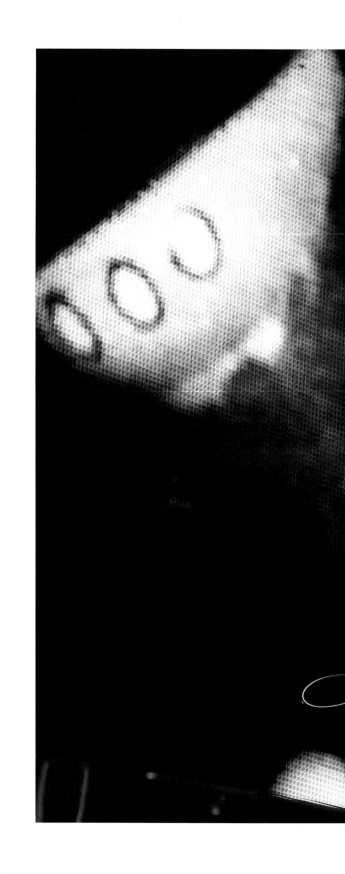

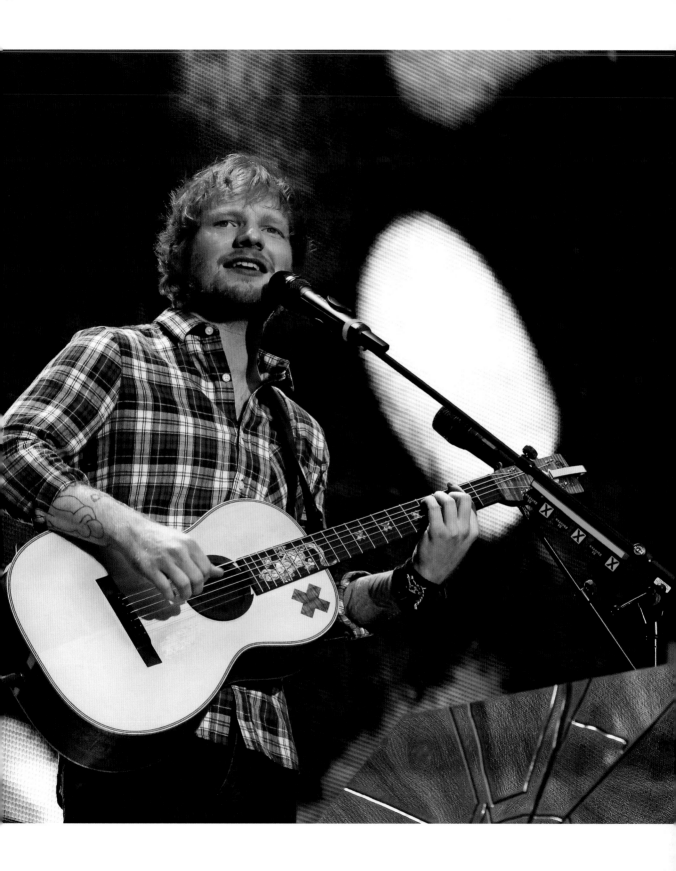

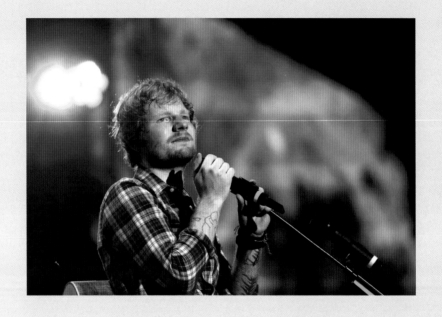

John Sheeran
This photo captures a moment of stillness and contemplation amid the euphoria of Ed's Wembley performance.

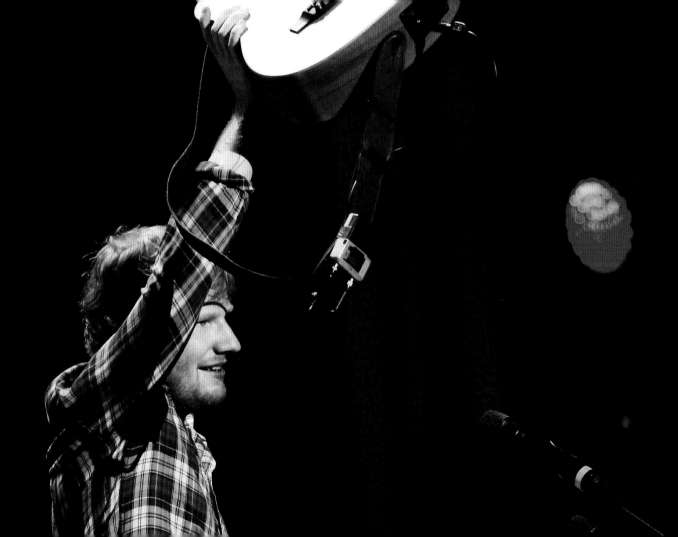

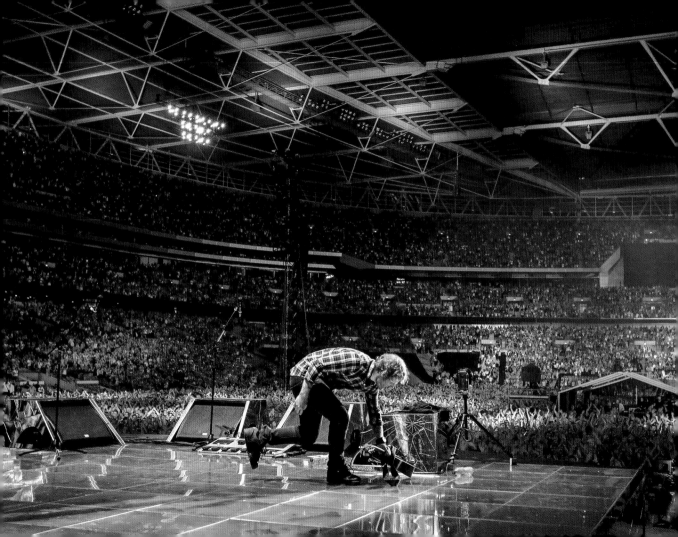

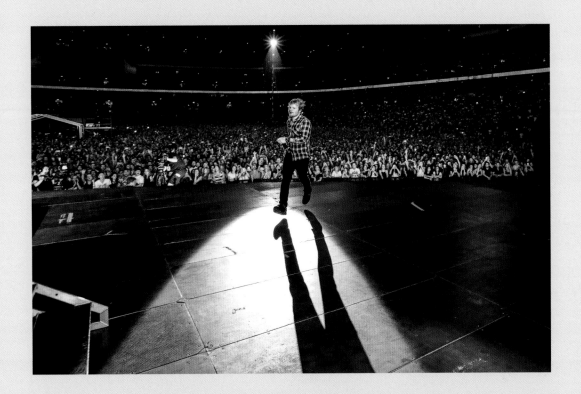

Christie Goodwin

This is my favourite picture of that evening at Wembley Stadium. It all seems pretty straightforward but nothing is what it seems. The spotlight behind Ed was constantly moving, and my aim was to capture Ed when that spot would be just at the right place so it would cast an almost perfect shadow on to the floor. The reason why I like this picture so much is that I did manage to get it right, with the spot draping a fine shadow across the floor, but while doing so I also caught Ed mid-air as if he is flying over the stage. I love it when things come together like this.

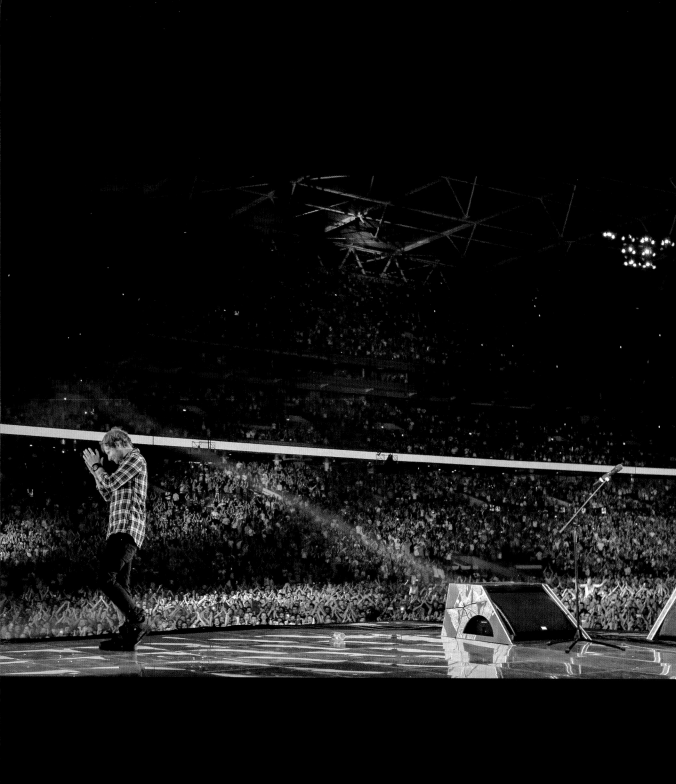

John Sheeran

It is the end of the show. Ed has the Wembley crowd singing and clapping. He is taking his leave and he has a broad smile on his face. Before he went onstage, his body language and his expression revealed his doubt and nerves. But it's all over now and he's proved to himself that he can do it, and he will be back for two more nights. The illuminated line that runs all the way around the inside of Wembley Stadium leads to his head and to his expression of relief and joy. Even one of the stage lights seems to follow and salute him.

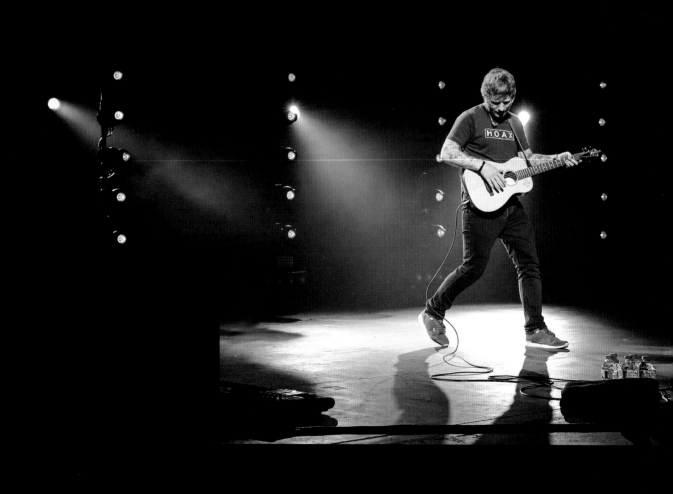

teenage cancer trust II

———

ON MY TURF AGAIN

It had been three years since Ed made his debut at the Royal Albert Hall as part of the Teenage Cancer Trust week in 2014. When I got the call that Ed would also be performing as part of the 2017 Teenage Cancer Trust shows I was raring to go. He'd only just started touring again earlier that month after a year's hiatus and this would be his first UK performance. Such fun!

When I arrived at the Albert Hall that evening, there was an unusually large crowd blocking the way to the stage door, so I had to battle my way through. Once inside, I picked up my pass from the reception desk and they told me that the reason for the crowd outside of their door was because there was a long list of VIP guests that night. It seemed that the Beckhams, Pippa Middleton and her now husband James Matthews, Michael McIntyre and James Blunt were all expected that evening. I mean, how these people acquire the knowledge that these guests are coming is beyond me.

As per usual, I went down to the artists' bar, which I always use as my makeshift office when working the Hall and set up my gear. Part of the bar was taken up by the people from the Teenage Cancer Trust. We moved some tables and chairs around and my office was all set. Outside the bar I could hear a lot of running around going on and you could just feel the excitement. In the corridors, I ran into Imogen and John Sheeran and we had a lovely chat.

About ten minutes before the show I descended the stairs to make my way to the pit. I hadn't done backstage shots. Ed's schedule was bonkers this time around: he had basically interrupted his European tour and just flown in from Berlin to do this charity show and was flying out immediately to continue his tour in Stockholm.

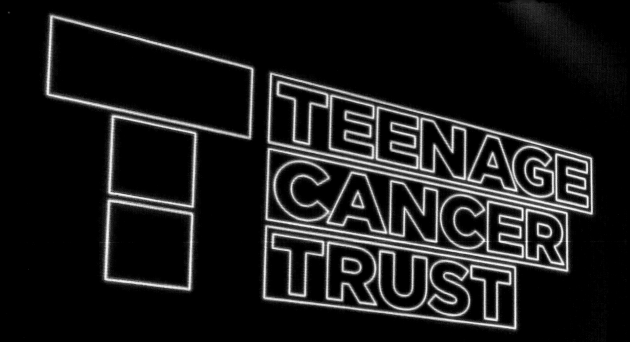

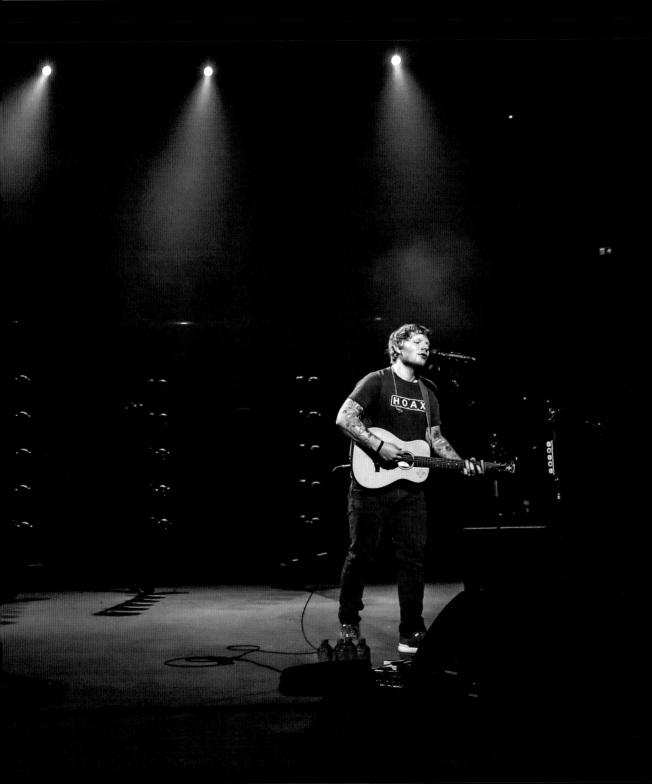

I looked around from down on the floor of the arena and the hall was just jam-packed and buzzing. For the opening act that evening we were treated to the boys of Busted. They are a lively bunch and I love shooting them, as you can always expect the unexpected. Earlier that day Busted had done a music workshop with teenagers from the Teenage Cancer Trust, assisted by members of the venue's own Albert's Band, and they spent the afternoon writing and making music together.

After the quick changeover, the Teenage Cancer Trust's patron Roger Daltrey walked onstage, joined by some of the workshop participants from earlier that day, to introduce Ed. Roger insisted that they take out their phones and use their moment onstage to take a selfie with the audience in the background. As I was standing in front of the first row, I must have been in all the selfies. I can only apologize for that.

Ed Sheeran appeared and started off his gig by telling the crowd he was going to treat the Royal Albert Hall like a scummy pub. Only Ed could get away with making such a statement in such a prestigious hall. He went on to perform songs from his album ÷, which he'd just released. He had the crowd singing along to every single word as per usual. I ran to the four corners of the hall and my Fitbit went well over the 10,000 steps I usually hit when I shoot a show at the Albert Hall. That night I broke all records and earned my "High Tops" badge, meaning I had walked twenty thousand steps in one day. Everywhere I popped up, the crowd was loud and wild.

There are five floors at the Royal Albert Hall, which means climbing a lot of stairs to get to the gallery at the top, to get those all-important bird's-eye shots. I used to take the elevator up but I got stuck in one of them once and missed a crucial guest appearance by an important artist onstage. So I avoid those elevators now. I'll give them a lingering look as I pass by and then climb the endless stairs to the fifth floor.

As I was dashing back down the majestic staircase to the lower levels, I literally ran over a woman who was climbing the stairs carrying flutes of champagne. It was one of those crashes where you feel you have no control over what is happening and you end up falling into each other's arms. Some of the champagne splashed out of the flutes and spilled on me in the process.

I apologized profusely, and she just looked at me with a calm, stoic glance and nodded that all was well. I continued my dash down the stairs two steps at a time and I just arrived at the side of the stage when Ed was taking his customary selfie with the crowd. It was the whole reason why I had been running so fast. I didn't want to miss that moment and I did capture it just in time. Ed walked off stage at the opposite side of me, doing the obligatory walk-off before coming back for the encore. Ed returned to the stage. For a split second our eyes met, he smiled and then walked to the front of the stage for the encore. He brought the evening to a perfect crescendo by beat-boxing "You Need Me, I Don't Need You". Every single person present in the hall was jumping up and down to the beat and I could feel a slight tremble under my feet caused by the mass foot stamping, a very, very rare thing at the Royal Albert Hall. To paraphrase Carole King, I felt the earth move under my feet as the evening drew to a close.

It was almost four o'clock in the morning when I had finally finished editing all my pictures of the night. As I flicked through my final selection one more time, I listened to my personal favourite Ed moment, his cover of Nina Simone's "Be My Husband". I'll let you in on a little secret. Whenever I edit a shoot, I put on one song on repeat, for hours and hours on end, the same song. And whether I edit an Ed Sheeran shoot or another shoot, that song is always my first choice.

While I got ready for bed, I heard my daughter waking up to get ready to go to work. What a weird life I lead, I thought to myself. But I wouldn't have it any other way.

John Sheeran

This is the second time that Christie photographed Ed at the Royal Albert Hall. She was determined to shoot him from many different spots around the famous arena. Here, Ed is in full flow with the audience. Above, the lighting display has a futuristic *Close Encounters* feel to it. It is as if a spacecraft has just dropped Ed on to the stage and has then taken off.

Overleaf

John Sheeran

A great shot of Ed, who is caught by the main spotlight that tracks his movement around the stage. His guitar-playing shadow is cast within an oval of brilliant light across the stage floor. And within the shadow there is a beautiful flickering of blue balls of light, like shimmering water.

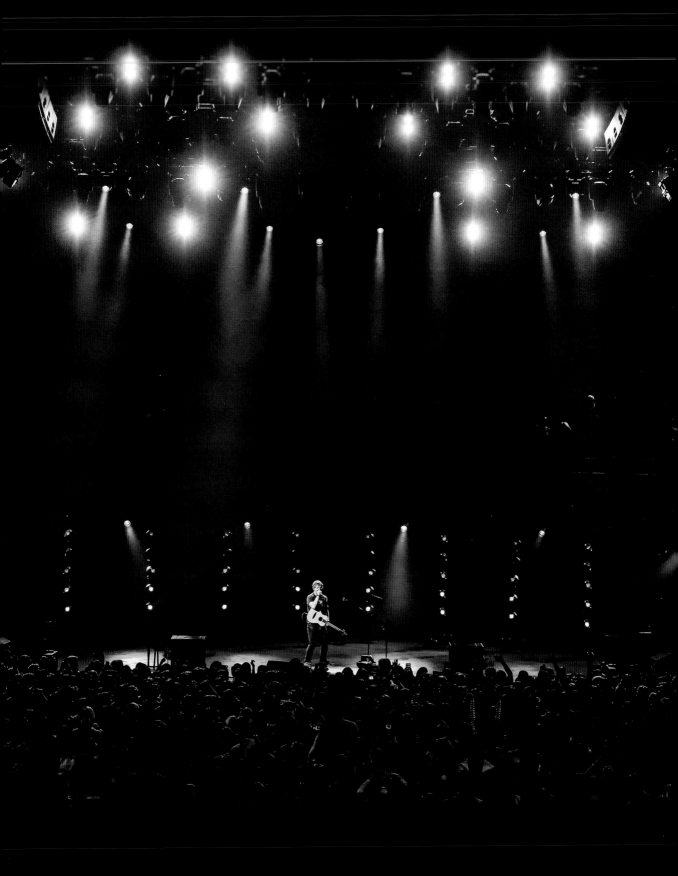

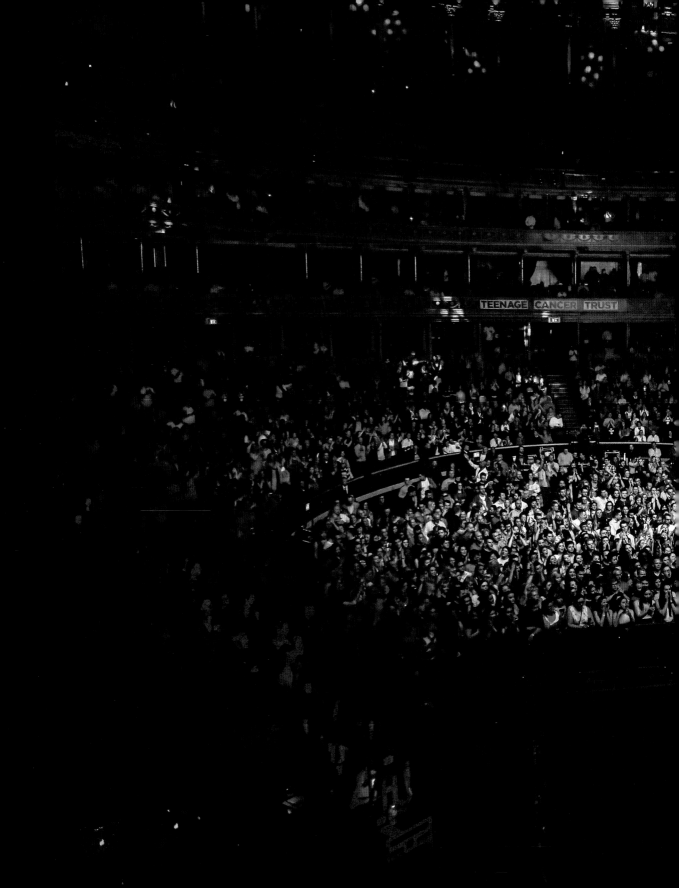

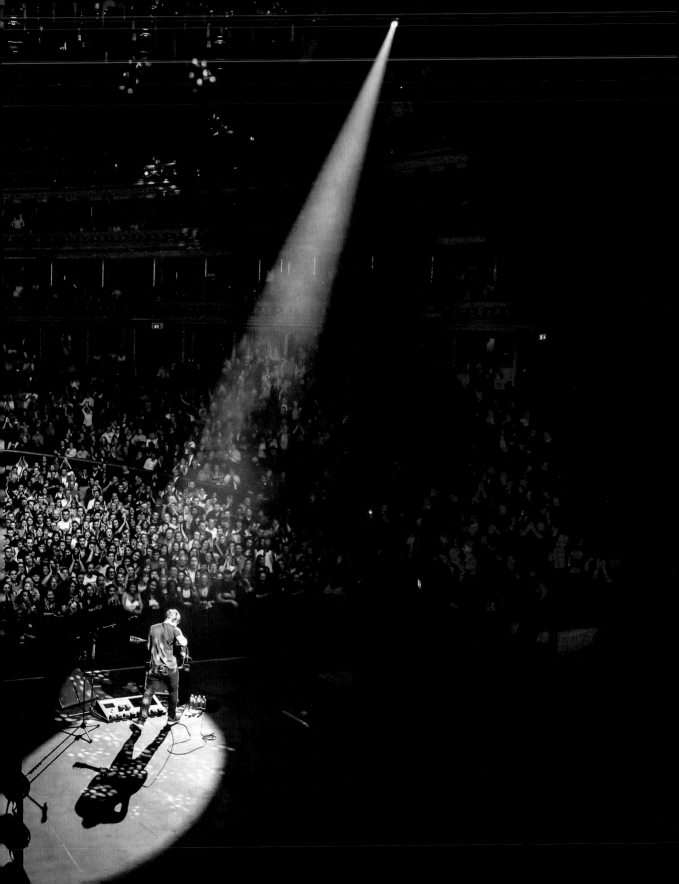

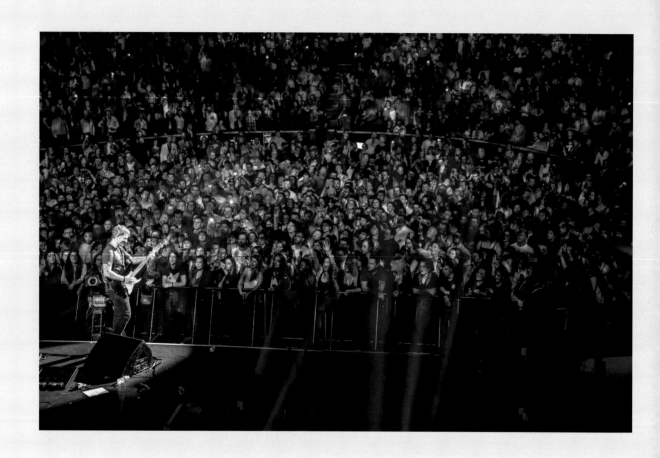

John Sheeran

Ed is pushed to one side in this composition, as Christie's interest is primarily focused on the crowd's reaction. The lights around the stage are turned on the audience. Ed is playing an electric guitar, with a smile on his face. I think he is probably playing the first few notes of his huge hit single "Thinking Out Loud". He smiles as he hears the reaction of those fans who instantly recognize the song he is about to sing.

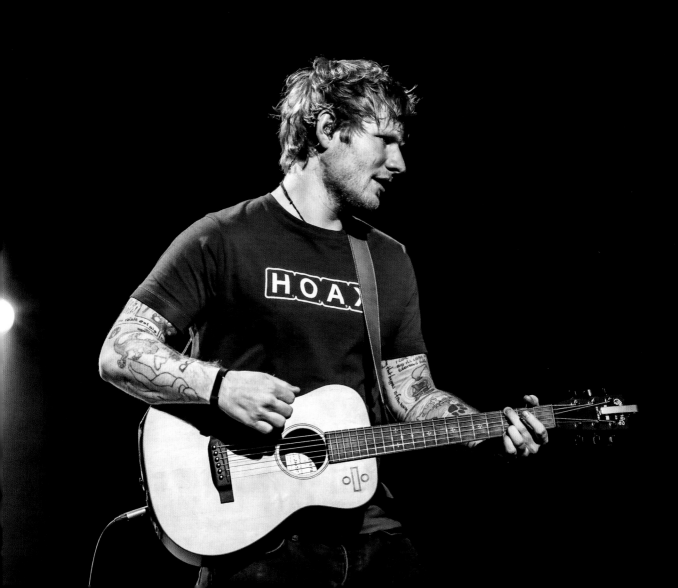

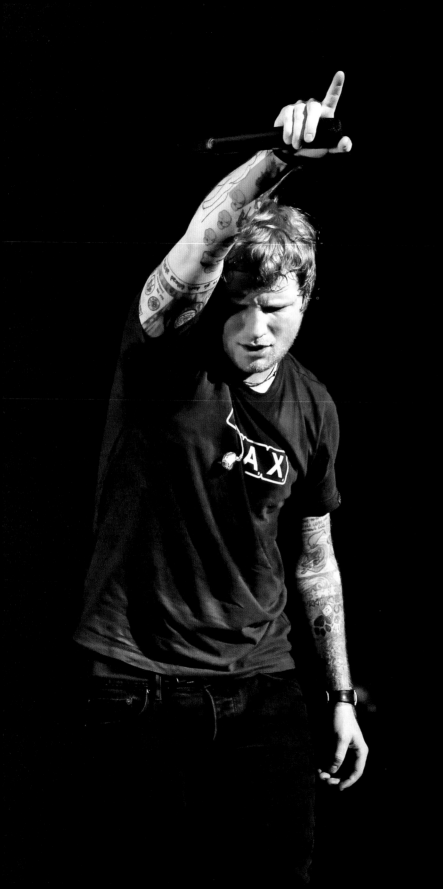

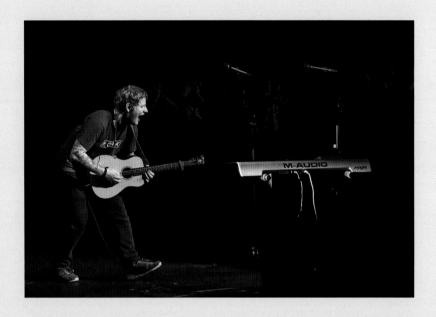

Christie Goodwin

This picture was taken from the stage at the Royal Albert Hall. I love it when there are pockets of light on the crowd, which I can incorporate into the picture. You see Ed enthusiastically rocking this song, and because of the perfect timing of the light pocket on the crowd you get an intimate moment between Ed and his fans.

John Sheeran

Here is another great shot of Ed at the Royal Albert Hall firing on all cylinders, with the audience reaction and participation captured like a frieze in the background. The keyboard is onstage, so this is probably toward the end of the gig, with Ed performing "Shape of You". I love that Ed can fill so many people with such a wide range of emotions during a gig. I have seen people overjoyed one minute and weeping the next.

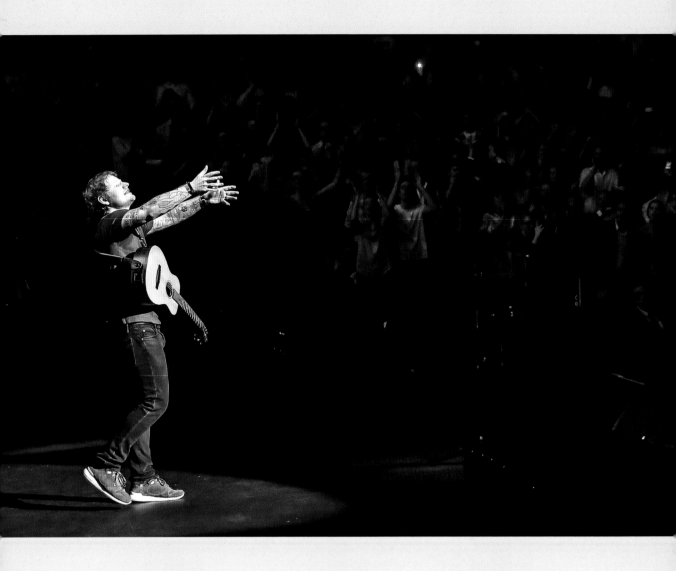

John Sheeran

Ed and his fans are fully engaged with each other. This is a climactic moment in his performance, but not everyone is so committed. Look at the bottom right and you will see a man in a suit and tie who looks disinterestedly at Ed. And next to him are a couple who are passively looking away in the opposite direction. Ed Sheeran's music isn't for them. They are here to support the Teenage Cancer Trust and seem prepared to tolerate, but not to participate.

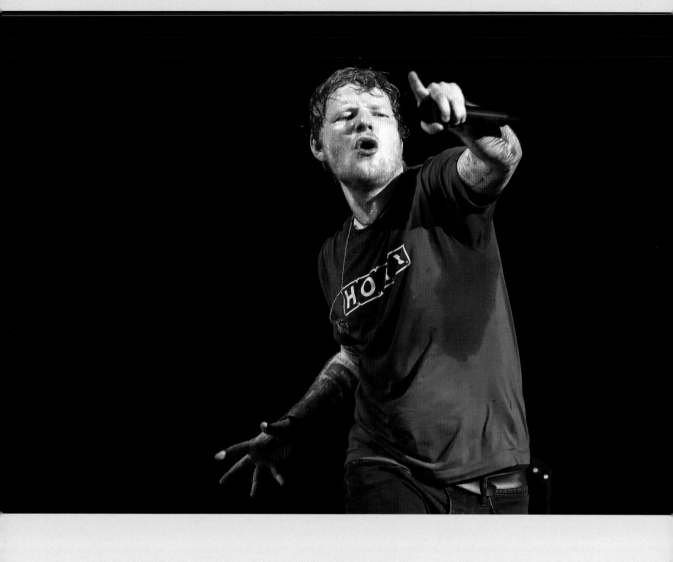

John Sheeran

This photo gives an excellent idea of just how physically exhausting one of Ed's gigs can be. His Hoax T-shirt is soaked with sweat and his head is dripping. The pose captured in this shot is like that of a Classical sculpture of an athlete. Typically, for Christie, there is nothing but the figure in the picture. The physicality of Ed's presence is remarkable.

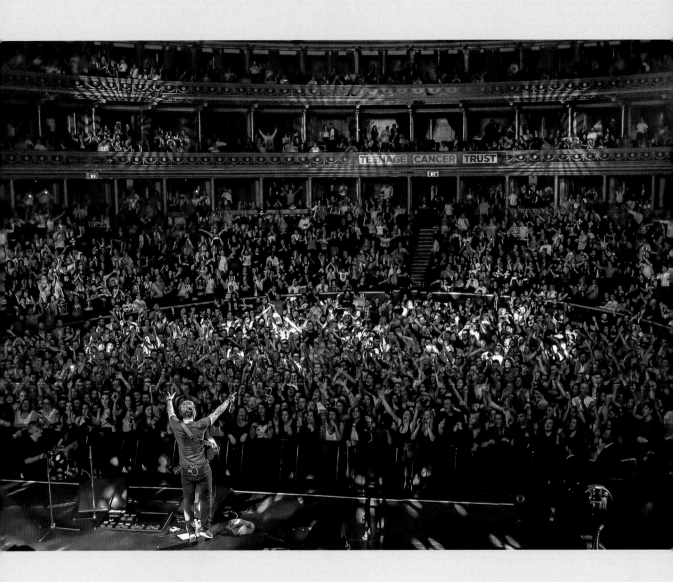

John Sheeran

It is as if Ed is conducting the Royal Albert Hall audience. The outstretched gestures and elated expressions of the crowd are reminiscent of a highly charged evangelical gathering.

afterword

— THE DIRTY TRUTH —

While flicking through the pictures in this book you might be wondering whether you too could pick up a camera and become a music photographer. When I'm in the pit waiting for the show to start, I am often asked by people in the front row how they could get into the pit because, let's be honest, it's a place where many would love to be. That's the lure of my job when you look in from the outside – the beguiling notion that you can stand almost within touching distance of those superstars and witness their performance up close and personal.

I'd like to share with you what my job in the pit really entails. A music photographer shoots live concerts and portraits of musicians. Some are there to shoot for media; a few might be working for the venue; one or two might be hired by the artist's management. During the 1950s and 1960s professional photographers were increasingly hired to cover concerts, and slowly but surely some photographers started specializing only in music. In the decades that followed popular music got bigger and more and more professional, and in the last decade or so the internet has exploded, with social media now driven by images. Professional music photography has changed with the times. Today those photographers you find in the pit mostly shoot for print or online media and are mostly freelancers with a day job. I shot a lot for the media at first, but these days many photographers are lucky to get a couple of pounds or dollars for a concert photo. I know – quite an eye opener, isn't it? I've always wanted to make a living as a photographer, so my aim from the start was to work for the artists themselves. That's what I do now. So how did I actually get here?

Back when I was studying photography, in my final year we had to present our work to an independent jury that not only judged your work but would also fire a collection of questions at you to see if you were industry ready. I must admit that I had dreaded that whole part of the circus because I'm not solid when

I am put on the spot. When I finally found myself in front of the firing squad, I was asked an array of questions about the work I was presenting. I thought I was doing well, until they threw a curveball at me: one of the jury members asked me what I wanted to achieve in my career after I left college. The question totally caught me off guard and I felt the floor sink from beneath me. My mind went blank. I truthfully didn't know what to say. All I wanted was to take pictures. A long awkward silence took hold of the room and the members of the jury in front of me were shifting uneasily in their chairs while I was racking my brain to come up with an answer.

All I could think of was a song I had heard on the radio before I had come to the interview. It was "The Cover of 'Rolling Stone'" by Dr. Hook & The Medicine Show. The chorus of that song kept repeating in my head, so that's what I said: "I want my picture on the cover of *Rolling Stone* magazine." The members of the jury were taken aback. They thought I was awfully ambitious setting such high goals. They gave me a glowing review for my presentation and ambition.

Looking back at it now I have to admit that, despite my little panic moment, I did have dreams and things I wanted to achieve. I had this wild dream of owning my own studio where I would be taking pictures all day long, with a backyard where I'd sit and drink wine with my friends while having deep intriguing philosophical conversations. I dreamed of having these elaborate and hugely successful exhibitions in all corners of the globe with rave reviews. Maybe I just wasn't ready yet to share my dreams with the world when I was asked that question.

As the years passed, I have never stopped dreaming. I have always wanted to be able to create images, to capture beauty, to chase that perfect picture.

Depending on whom you ask, success means different things. If you were to ask me, I'd say it means turning my passion into a successful career. The first step in achieving success is to establish what success means to you. Everyone has a talent, something they are really good at. You just have to find yours and put in the effort to make yourself better at it. Set goals, and set them high, much higher than seems realistic. You also need to be really passionate because just talent without any passion is a bit like a car without fuel.

I was often told that I was wasting my time trying to achieve success with my work. People will always try to put you down. Dreaming is often considered a waste of time. The truth of the matter is that the first step to achieving success is to envision it. And for every hour you spend envisioning your success you may come one step closer to actually reaching it. So, to anyone out there who has a dream: dream, dream, dream your dreams. They are the foundations of your career. But they are useless without persistence. Many times I was driven to the brink of desperation and was ready to give up photography. Just like Ed when he first started out must have had moments, too, when he thought he was getting nowhere, but he just persisted. Talent alone won't cut it. You need passion to fuel it; you need bravery to accept failure. Failure is not only inevitable, but a necessary step on your way to success. Just like Ed at one time had a dream to reach an audience with his music, to touch people with his lyrics, to be able to collaborate with people he admired. Today there aren't enough adjectives to describe the measure of his success. He's got his awards, he's got his MBE, he's got his sold-out tours, he's done his list of impressive collaborations. I've heard the critics on the sidelines saying that it all came quite easy to him. But, take it from me, Ed's success was achieved by sheer determination, with a lot of hardship and falling and getting back up on the pony.

So, I had my *Rolling Stone* dream and a degree, and almost immediately life took me somewhere else entirely. It took me 25 years of shooting pretty much everything apart from music, and not chasing my goals at all, to finally wake up and pursue my old dream with everything I had. More than ever before people told me I was nuts. I knocked on doors and begged for photo passes. Most doors stayed closed, some opened, and I kept knocking. I shot a lot in clubs and did a lot of heavy metal gigs at first (for some reason, it was easier to get a photo pass at metal festivals). I learned how to shoot concerts, how to feel the show as much as hear it, how to shoot in low light conditions. I have never stopped studying and experimenting since my first days at college. I know my cameras inside out. I learned how to use Lightroom, my favourite editing software. I kept my portfolio updated, invested in a decent website, did anything I could to get shoots and get my work seen. And eventually more doors opened.

It all seems pretty straightforward but there is a dirty truth. Music photography is one of the toughest fields to make a living in. Pretty much all other fields of photography are more lucrative. So, unless you have a real passion for this one, don't even think about it. For those very few who are able to do this as a full-time job, it's a tough lifestyle. It's not nine-to-five days, five days a week with the weekends off. When you're on a job, it's often 20 hours a day, and when you're on a tour, there are no days off, because when the artist isn't performing, I'm still editing. So there's no social life outside the music bubble, and you can't really plan much ahead because in most cases the photographer is hired last, not first. Most jobs tend to be last-minute calls. My first really big tour was the European leg of Usher's OMG tour in 2011. His then manager, Rob Hallett, called us, and asked if we were free for two months and whether we could be on a plane the next day to Berlin. That is the nature of the business.

There's no job security in music photography, and actually the same goes for most people in music in general. You have to constantly knock on doors, sell yourself, negotiate, and understand that it will take a few hundred "no thank yous" (and a few hundred more "no replies") before you get that first big "yes". There have been periods in my career when I was staring into a great dark void, with no commissions for months ahead. In the first couple of years, while still mainly shooting in clubs and at metal festivals, I've worked at a cancer research centre, and have been a personal assistant to a rabbi and personal assistant to a lawyer in London. A girl's gotta do what a girl's gotta do to make ends meet.

Once you are on the job, it involves a lot of waiting and just hanging around. You don't know when you'll get an opportune moment to shoot. We call it "hurry up and wait". I have spent more time sitting on flight cases in a backstage corridor than I care to remember. I have fallen asleep on them, too. They don't roll out a red carpet for you when you get on a tour. The artist and the touring crew work their butts off every day and night, often getting by with just a couple of hours of sleep in a bunk on a bus that is less comfortable than most coffins, all so that the audience can have those magical two hours every night. It involves a lot of logistics, unexpected problems and teamwork to put it all in place. My advice to you is to never forget that you are "only" a photographer because in all honesty, everyone from management to the catering staff is so much more important than you are because they all work towards that one goal: put on the best show ever. You're just there to capture the fruits of their hard work.

So why am I still doing this after knowing and living the dirty truth, day in and day out? I can honestly tell you that there have been many moments throughout my career that I have asked myself that very question, but then ... the music starts and the crowd cheers, and the adrenaline starts pumping through my veins. The singer grabs the mic and right there in that moment I feel happy, I feel secure, I feel content, I feel like I can conquer it all, and I wouldn't change it for the world.

about the authors

―――――

CHRISTIE GOODWIN

Christie Goodwin is a British photographer with a career that spans over 35 years. She first picked up the camera at the age of 12. After obtaining a bachelor's degree in art photography, she initially shot fashion assignments but soon got restless and left the fashion world behind her.

After getting married and starting a family, she decided to return to what she had studied. For a good decade, she shot mainly fine art projects and held regular exhibitions to showcase her work. At the turn of the century Christie took on regular assignments to shoot political news as an editorial photographer for wire agencies.

It wasn't until 2005 when she was commissioned to shoot a live performance that she found her true calling. After that first assignment, she hung up her editorial hat and became a full-time music and entertainment photographer. Today Christie is in high demand as a tour and portrait photographer. She has worked for Ed Sheeran, Katy Perry, Taylor Swift, One Direction, Paul McCartney, Rod Stewart and other top recording artists. Christie's work appears on CDs, DVDs and tour merchandise, and in international publications, books and exhibitions. Fast, creative and a little bit crazy, Christie is known and respected for always getting the shot and for her no-nonsense approach when connecting with the artist.

When not on the road in a tour bus, Christie is at home in London, where she regularly shoots as official photographer for the Royal Albert Hall. She also shoots covers for best-selling crime novels.

Christie hates free time, unless she can spend it in France ... preferably with a camera. She can be found on both instagram and twitter, @christiegoodwin.

JOHN SHEERAN

John Sheeran is the father of Ed Sheeran. He has worked for over 35 years in the arts, as a curator, exhibition organizer and lecturer.

John worked as a museum curator during the 1980s, including seven years as curator of Dulwich Picture Gallery, London. At Dulwich, he was responsible for a world famous collection of Old Master paintings and a Sir John Soane architectural masterpiece. He also established the gallery's first exhibition and education programmes.

In 1990, John left museums to set up the art consultancy Sheeran Lock with his wife Imogen. Over the next 20 years, they organized national and international art exhibitions and art education projects. In 1998, John curated *Travels with the Prince* at Hampton Court Palace, which celebrated Prince Charles's 50th birthday and featured his private art collection from his country home, Highgrove. In 2000, John curated *Our World in the Year 2000*, the United Nations' millennium exhibition. This showed paintings by 250 artists from around the world. It was held at UN Headquarters in New York and opened by then UN secretary-general Kofi Annan.

During his time at Sheeran Lock, John ran a consultancy service for professional artists, advising many painters, sculptors and printmakers on their career development and direction. He also organized innovative art education projects in schools throughout the UK, including *Talking Pictures* and *Pride of Place*. In 2006, he curated *Young Brits at Art* at the Royal Albert Hall, London, for the UK's Commission for Racial Equality.

In 2008, John began to give art lectures in Suffolk, where he lives. His first series, *Discover the Great Painters*, comprised 80 lectures on Western European artists from the 13th century to the present. Later series included *Great Cities of Art* and *Masterpiece*.

First published in Great Britain in 2018 by Cassell, a division of
Octopus Publishing Group Ltd.

Text and illustrations copyright © Lakotah Ltd 2018
Design and layout copyright © Octopus Publishing Ltd 2018

HarperCollins books may be purchased for educational, business, or sales promotional use.
For information please email the Special Markets Department at SPsales@harpercollins.com.

Published in 2018 by
Harper Design
An Imprint of HarperCollins *Publishers*
195 Broadway
New York, NY 10007
Tel: (212) 207-7000
Fax: (855) 746-6023
harperdesign@harpercollins.com
www.hc.com

Distributed throughout North America by
HarperCollins *Publishers*
195 Broadway
New York, NY 10007

Library of Congress Control Number: 2018944028

ISBN 978-0-06-288326-1

Printed in China

Commissioning editor: Joe Cottington
Senior editor: Pauline Bache
Copy editor: Robert Anderson
Creative director: Jonathan Christie
Designer: Jeremy Tilston
Senior production controller: Allison Gonsalves

Cover design: Jeremy Tilston and Sarah Gifford

THANK YOU, MERCI, DANKE, GRACIAS, DANK U

I'd like to thank my manager and partner Patrick Cusse for believing in me and getting me here. And I'm glad we could finally tick this one off your bucket list – you are welcome. Thank you to Joe Cottington and the Octopus Publishing team for jumping on board with this crazy idea. Thank you to Carrie Kania and Iconic Images for making things happen – you were the first to say "Let's do this". I would also like to thank my family and all my friends, virtual and real, for always supporting me. Thank you to all the artists I have ever worked with – you've all helped me get better. Thank you Simon Porter for giving me my first job as a music photographer. Thank you Roy Weissman and Joe Bonamassa for your friendship and for always pushing me to be more creative. Love and gratitude to Baron Wolman who has always been an inspiration and a great friend. A massive cheer and a heartfelt thank you to Stuart Camp and Mark Friend who've always been so helpful and supportive. Thank you Imogen Sheeran for your friendship and continuous support … and I just love your jewellery. Thank you Ed Sheeran just for being you. Thank you John Sheeran. You've been my partner in crime in this project and I couldn't have done it without your wise counsel and expertise. I'll be forever grateful. Thank you to my son Charlie for always challenging me to be more creative. And, last but not least, thank you to my daughter, Robbin – you've been there for me every step of the way.